· The Virgin and the Bride ·

THE VIRGIN
AND THE BRIDE

*Idealized Womanhood
in Late Antiquity*

KATE COOPER

HARVARD UNIVERSITY PRESS

Cambridge, Massachusetts

London, England

First Harvard University Press paperback edition, 1999

Library of Congress Cataloging-in-Publication Data

Cooper, Kate, 1960–
    The virgin and the bride : idealized womanhood in late antiquity /
Kate Cooper.
       p. cm.
    Includes bibliographical references and index.
    ISBN 0-674-93949-2 (cloth)
    ISBN 0-674-93950-6 (pbk.)
    1. Latin literature—History and criticism. 2. Women and
literature—Rome—History. Christian literature, Early—Latin
authors—History and criticism. 4. Christianity and literature—
Rome—History. 5. Rome—History—Empire, 30 B.C.–600 A.D.
6. Christian women saints in literature. 7. Literature and society—
Rome—History. 8. Married women in literature. 9. Social values
in literature. 10. Virginity in literature. 11. Women in
literature. 12. Women—Rome—History. I. Title.
PA6030.W7C67   1996
870.9′352042—dc20   96-2256

For Conrad

· Contents ·

Preface

This book proposes a fresh answer to one of the most interesting questions of ancient history: why did the early Christians alight on the ideal of virginity, and why did the Romans come to adopt it as their own, even when they saw that its triumph would undermine the very fabric of ancient society? It is a question that has troubled the historical profession since Gibbon, and no satisfactory answer has yet been found.

The attempt here has been to take the question from an unexpected point of view. Instead of focusing on the innovators, the Christians themselves, I have tried to imagine the outlook of the literate Roman, to understand how she or he would have perceived the questions of sexual morality and religious allegiance at stake in such a dramatic change. The reason for the Christians' seemingly inexplicable success seems to lie in the way the political and moral theorists of the Roman empire understood the relationship of sexual morality to civic virtue. Unwittingly, they had left an unstable link in the system for judging a man's fitness for public office. Enormous symbolic importance was vested in his private life and his susceptibility to womanly influence, a point which may sound disarmingly familiar to modern readers. The weakness of this system was that it privileged sexual self-restraint as an index of moral authority at the same time as public men were encouraged to father legitimate heirs as vigorously as they could. The early Christians broke the paradox by picturing their own moral heroes as men who eschewed earthly heirs for an otherworldly family, and won the empire itself for their pains. The female figure of the virgin was the cultural icon by which they broadcast their message.

A few readers will be disappointed that I have steered clear of some of the more familiar landmarks: for example, to mention only the most glaring omission, the Virgin Mary has no place here, despite the rise of her cult precisely during the period under study. I have tried resolutely to cleave to the unfamiliar as a starting point, and to the perspective of the kind of ancient person who, while serious enough in his or her ethical commitments, was not given to religious enthusiasms. What would she, or he, have thought of the changing dynamics of gender, sexual morality, and religious ideology brought on by the rise of Christianity?

While I have tried to give even attention, insofar as possible, to pagan and Christian points of view, I should offer two caveats. The first is that I have consistently used the term "pagan" despite the fact that it is anachronistic and inexact. The pagans thought of themselves as "Romans," "Hellenes," "followers of religion"—all terms that might also, in some circumstances, describe a Jew or a Christian—but they simply did not think the Jews or Christians important enough to invent a name for members of their society who had nothing in common other than the fact that they did not worship the God of Israel. Similarly, I have referred to "the Christians" where it is clear that there were numerous opposing definitions of Christianity, many of whose adherents rejected one another as heretical or not Christian at all. This causes particular difficulty when we come to the late fourth century when many Christians, long dismissed by historians as "half-hearted" because they rejected the self-righteousness of certain proponents of virginity, may in fact have held tolerance and religious pluralism to be an aspect of the Christian virtue of charity.

I have tried to cast this study in terms that would be accessible to a broad readership whose primary interest might be in history, gender studies, classics, or religion, to name only the most obvious areas. This cross-disciplinary approach has many advantages, and I hope it allows me to tell a story that offers unexpected insights to all concerned. At the same time, it has the disadvantage that if I were to present at every point the documentation and scholarly debate which each specialist in turn might crave, the specialists from other areas, not to mention the student or general reader, would find it difficult going. Because of this, the notes have been kept to a minimum, in part by the practice of limiting successive references to the same primary source to an indication in the main body of the text of the section number from which the particular quotation is drawn. Similarly, the bibliography refers only to the primary sources and secondary literature cited in the text, rather than to the broader reading that has influenced my thinking. Where I have cited from an existing translation of a text I have given the source at the first citation; otherwise, all translations are my own.

Just as a book reflects a lifetime of reading, so it is an attempt to capture an echo of evenings and afternoons spent in conversation, of letters exchanged, of ideas discovered and defended among friends. Although none bears responsibility for shortcomings the reader may find in what follows, I owe a great many debts to the colleagues whose delight in ancient history has sustained my own. The first is to John Gager, Janet Martin, and Peter Brown, who jointly supervised the doctoral dissertation at Princeton University from which this book, somewhat obliquely, draws its origin. To the last, I owe a special debt of gratitude for taking pains well beyond the call of duty.

I am similarly grateful to a small band of scholars writing in the area of gender in late antiquity who have read part or all of the manuscript, and who have often made available to me works in progress of their own: Virginia Burrus, Susanna Elm, Simon Goldhill, Vasiliki Limberis, and Judith Perkins. Of this group, Elizabeth Clark and Averil Cameron are to be thanked not only for thoughtful criticism but also for the leadership which they have provided for a generation of younger scholars. Others have read drafts of part or all of the book and have helped me to understand the broader context into which the study fits: Mary Douglas, Leigh Gibson, Judith Herrin, David Hunter, Ann Kuttner, Robert Lamberton, Henrietta Leyser, Felice Lifshitz, Richard Lim, Robert Markus, John Petruccione, Francesco Scorza Barcellona, Jeffrey Stout, Andrew Wallace-Hadrill, and Vincent Wimbush. I owe warm thanks to Herbert Bloch for a memorable afternoon spent discussing the funerary inscriptions of Fabia Aconia Paulina and Vettius Agorius Praetextatus, and to Robbi and Kent Cooper for constantly asking hard questions.

A number of institutions provided the financial support without which this study could never have been undertaken, much less completed. The Episcopal Church Foundation and the Charlotte W. Newcombe Fellowship administered by the Woodrow Wilson Foundation supported the dissertation out of which it grew. The Dumbarton Oaks Byzantine Library supported three invaluable months of research in its collections in the summer of 1990. The American Academy in Rome offered a year of intellectual bliss shuttling back and forth among the incomparable libraries of Rome, including its own. I am also grateful to the Department of Religion at Barnard College, Columbia University, my academic home during the period when the manuscript was completed, and to its chair, John Stratton Hawley, for encouragement, toleration, and warm collegiality.

Material from Chapter 6 was published in *Modelli di comportamento e modelli di santità,* ed. Giulia Barone, Marina Caffiero, and Francesco Scorza Barcellona (Turin: Rosenberg and Sellier, 1994). I am grateful to the publisher for permission to reprint it here.

Finally, I have relied on the wisdom and sense of humor of one indispensable critic, editor, and interlocutor: my husband, Conrad Leyser. In more ways than can be catalogued, this book is the fruit of our trustful partnership, and it is to him that I dedicate it, with heartfelt thanks.

· 1 ·

Private Lives, Public Meanings

"The first without compunction violates his wife, his serving-women, and his attendants, whether young *(paedagogia, capillati)* or old *(exoleti)*; the second, no longer having the power to give orders outside, in the wider society, no longer has the strength to give them at all: of necessity, he invents for himself a conjugal and sexual morality."[1]

With this memorable characterization of the psychology of the Roman senator before and after the Augustan revolution, Paul Veyne introduced, nearly twenty years ago, the notion that it was not compassionate Christian apostles but dispirited pagan senators who first proposed a moral dimension to the exercise of patriarchal power in the ancient world, an easing of the austere idea of family life that had prevailed in the Roman republic. Veyne's purposes were frankly polemical. He felt that the early Christians had been given credit for a moral legacy when in fact Christianity was not responsible and the legacy was not necessarily good.

No concession was to be made to the self-interested rationalizations offered by latterday apologists for early Christianity, but neither did heroes emerge on the side of the pagans. A change had indeed taken place around the turn of the eras, and its architect was not Jesus but Augustus. Yet the change was merely an unintended by-product of the Roman Senate's cowardice in facing a single man's claim to dominance. Put simply, the male Roman aristocrat had invented a rhetoric of con-

1

jugal love to compensate for his emasculation in the public realm. This was explained as an attempt to elicit affection from his wife as from his inferiors, where before he had exacted fearful subservience.

Having lost his standing in public, Veyne argued, the exemplary Roman man no longer had heart for the routine domestic self-assertion of an earlier age, when patriarchs had been known unflinchingly to hand over spouses and offspring to capital punishment, and their license to punish as they saw fit within the household was virtually limitless.[2] So the now-compromised public figure settled down in private to cultivate affectionate ties with those he had once dominated: the Roman ideal of love within marriage was born. The mitigation of patriarchal dominance was not only not a triumph of early Christian ethics; it was no triumph at all. This reading was Nietzschean in its irony. If the argument was undermined by a diffuse and unsystematic treatment of the evidence drawn from ancient sources,[3] it was carried by the quasi-pornographic magnetism both of the sources themselves and of Veyne's alarming sympathy for the psychology of sexual dominance.

Veyne's argument was compounded dramatically by its influence on Michel Foucault, then at work on his monumental *History of Sexuality*.[4] Foucault adapted Veyne's psychosexual insight into the aristocratic Roman man in the direction of a fully psychologized reading of the ancient idea of *erōs*. For Foucault, the period from Augustus to Marcus Aurelius was distinguished by anxiety about pleasure and domination in the minds of eminent men. A secure sense of the right to exact submission (including sexual submission) from one's subordinates had given way to an uneasy consciousness of one's own duties to others. The philosophical ideal came to rest in marriage as a friendship of equals, the result of a transfusion of aristocratic *maîtrise de soi* from the task of controlling others to that of fulfilling their expectations.

Much is owed to both writers by any subsequent traveler into the cultural territory they charted.[5] What follows will engage only indirectly with their work. But their vivid evocations of the contours of the ancient imagination have exerted such influence that the reader may find it useful to know in advance what major differences in the landscape this book will find.

Most important, while a watershed is still in view between the classical and the early medieval aristocrat's language for describing marriage and sexuality, the decisive change of terrain has moved again, back to the later Roman empire, although it no longer takes the shape of the triumph of early Christian ethics that Veyne labored so heroically to dislodge. Veyne saw the transformation of marriage as unrelated to religious change, where his predecessors had been inclined to see it as the inevitable result of Christianization. We will see that, over the first few centuries of the common era, pagans and Christians alike drew on a moral language of marital concord that had existed at least from the time of Augustus. The watershed lies in the introduction of an apologetic language of Christian moral superiority which deliberately misrepresented Christians as standing apart from this moral consensus. I will argue that this misrepresentation would have been understood by ancient readers as a distortion of reality for the purposes of argument.

Throughout this book an unfamiliar coloring has also been applied to the conventions of representation. The emphasis is on self-presentation as a medium for negotiating one's standing within a social group. The conventions by which literary and philosophical discussions of marital harmony reflected—or attempted to influence—social reality were governed at least in part by the self-interest of the speaker, a point that seems at times to have escaped Veyne and Foucault. Philosophers might debate the best view of marriage not because of a change in the structure of the aristocratic family but because of a jostling for position among schools.[6] Emperors would make known (or invent) an ideal of the imperial family's harmony as a vital component in the propaganda of imperial power.[7]

The representation of marital concord served an important rhetorical function, supporting the claims put forward by aristocratic men in competition with one another by implying their ethical fitness for responsibility. This rhetorical economy had cultural roots at least as old as the *Odyssey*. Men's struggle with one another for dominance was abetted by the suggestion of each that his own household was known for its concord while the other's was not. Equally, it was well understood that a man's claim to power was in fact a claim on behalf of his household and family line.

The decisive shift at the end of antiquity was not a change in the social reality of aristocratic marriage,[8] but the introduction of a competing moral language, the Christian rhetoric of virginity. The social and cultural repercussions of this challenge to rhetorical convention—its admission of a new group of men to a new kind of power—will be explored in detail in the chapters that follow.

Finally, the issue of gender receives explicit attention in these pages, as it did not in the work of Veyne and Foucault. There is no need to add here to the well-deserved criticism of Foucault for attempting to frame a history of sexuality without reference to the experience or self-understanding of the female part of the human race.[9] But my task is to integrate attention to gender even if it is only intermittently possible to approach the problem of female experience, a limitation imposed by the scarcity of first-hand accounts (and even of second-hand descriptions before the late fourth century). An attempt to understand the conventions by which gender-specific characteristics were assigned to women and to men, and the rhetorical ends that such conventions could serve, will tell us something about the relations between men and women, and at least as much again about the competition for power between men and other men. Again, the focus is on representation.

Where Foucault's *History of Sexuality* emphasized anxiety about pleasure, what follows will emphasize concern for self-representation. Just as our distinction between "public" and "private" might have baffled ancient men and women accustomed to perceiving the household as both the index and the end of men's struggle for position within the city, so their distinction between "rhetoric" and "reality" would have been constructed very differently from ours. In a society premised on honor and shame, rhetoric *was* reality.

This means that the symbolic language of gender would not have been internalized in the way a modern reader might expect. The male and female members of a household would have been seen, and would have understood themselves, as two representative dimensions, two *personae*, by which a household might project its quality and claim its rightful standing. If selfhood was, as is suggested here, understood through identification with family honor, its gender construction would have functioned very differently from that of an atomistic modern society. The quasi-Victorian notion of the private sphere which informs much contemporary writing on gender does little to render the self-understanding of the members of an ancient household. The key tension explored in our ancient texts is the tension between the interests of the household and those of the city.

Private Pleasures and the Public Man

Plutarch, whose writings in the late first and early second centuries figure significantly in Foucault's *History of Sexuality*, remains a virtually unexplored source of information on the crafting of public men's reputations by a deft use of gender-related conventions and commonplaces. His dictum that wives should follow their husbands' choice of gods is well known,[10] but his substantive illustrations of how concord between man and wife served as an emblem of *sōphrosynē*, the self-mastery that made men reliable citizens, have yet to be studied. Plutarch is a particularly rich source on this matter because of the link between his philosophical investigations and his historical writings. The treatment of a single area in both genres by the same author allows us privileged access to the question of how philosophy reflected the concrete social conditions chronicled by the historian. Thus the ideal of marital concord appears simultaneously in Plutarch's writings as a rhetorical motif in the politics of self-representation and as a narrative resolution for the philosophical problem of pleasure and instability.

In his *Erōtikos*, Plutarch reviews the philosophical lore on pleasure and reputation, engaging the seriousness of the debate on the pleasures without missing its humor.[11] What he emphasizes is the question of male self-control and trustworthiness. The dialogue is designed as a reenactment of Plato's *Symposium* and its debate over the relationship between the spiritually ennobling pursuit of the beautiful and the passionate urges of the body. Plutarch mocks Plato's idea that the philosopher can be induced to renounce pleasure in favor of a transcendent *erōs:* the pursuit of such an ideal can only result in hypocrisy.[12] Instead, the man of reason will acknowledge the inevitable and find a way to put pleasure at the service of philosophy. We will see later that Plutarch is the first in a tradition of ironic restagings of the *Symposium* and its debate on desire.

Plutarch's ironic view of the debate appears in the very setting of his dialogue: while Plato's *Symposium* takes its occasion from a banquet in praise of the god Eros, the story that frames the *Erōtikos* is an instance of *erōs* gone awry. Ismenodora, a wealthy widow, has been asked by the family of the noble youth Bacchon to find him an appropriate bride. The difference in age that disqualifies Ismenodora herself as a bride for the boy qualifies her as a matrimonial go-between, but a cross-gender intrigue develops as Ismenodora's sexual interest in Bacchon is criticized by her male age-peers, who themselves are attracted to the boy. Having fallen in love with her charge, Ismenodora abandons her duties on behalf of his family and kidnaps the boy with a view to marrying him herself. This mix-up provides a parodic introduction to the thesis that the pursuit of private desires endangers the fulfillment of social contracts. Yet, while Ismenodora's passion furnishes the comic impetus of the dialogue, Plutarch is not so much concerned with female desire as with male desire: with passion as a corridor through which objects of desire exert power over men. The ostensible interest in Ismenodora's agency as a desiring subject clothes an investigation of women as objects of desire.

It is in an atmosphere of pleasant raillery that two camps of Bacchon's middle-aged male friends take up the question of desire and pleasure, one group arguing for pederasty as the ideal form of *erōs* (because, according to the Platonic view, it scorns pleasure as it pursues the Beautiful), and the other arguing that heterosexual love is more sublime because it allows for the union of Aphrodite (goddess of the pleasures) and Eros. Plutarch clearly favors the second view. The character who serves as the author's spokesman[13] explains that the Platonic construction of pleasure and desire assumes that the only love object able to inspire the *erōs* that enables the soul is the kind of young man whose dignity would be violated were he pressed to serve another's pleasure (*Erōtikos* 768E). Here Plutarch sees the irony of a sexuality defined by dominance, so that only one partner can take pleasure at a time, and offers his own solution to the conundrum. For a man to take pleasure with his own wife is certainly licit and congruent with female nature, which is defined as being able to experience sexual submission without dishonor. So men might reconcile pleasure and ennobling friendship through conjugal love if they would perceive women's capacity for spiritual excellence (and thus for friendship). Even the beloved's power to beguile the lover could serve the purpose of philosophy:

Just as poetry, adding to prose meaning the delights of song and meter and rhythm, makes its educational power more forceful and its capacity for doing harm more irresistible; just so has nature endowed woman with charm of aspect, persuasiveness of voice, and seductive physical beauty, and has thus given the licentious woman great advantages for pleasure and deceit, but to the chaste *(tēi sōphroni)*, great resources also for gaining the goodwill and friendship of her husband. (*Erōtikos* 769B-C)

Plutarch suggests that pleasure does persuade, but to see its persuasion as necessarily evil is to miss an opportunity for promoting the common good.

At stake here is the ability of the beloved to sway the lover by charm (and the promise of sexual pleasure) rather than by reason. Plutarch takes the position that the wise man's strategy should be to find a loveable wife and teach her philosophy. In this way, the inevitable influence of pleasure will be an influence on behalf of philosophy rather than against it, exactly the view Plutarch offers when it comes to giving practical advice on how to educate a young wife in his *Conjugal Precepts*. The like-mindedness of man and wife becomes the guarantee of philosophy's place in the household. To support this harnessing of conjugal pleasures to high purpose, Plutarch invokes the legislation of Solon prescribing sexual intercourse between spouses at least once every ten days, "as cities from time to time renew their treaties by a libation" (*Erōtikos* 769B).

In Plutarch's *Parallel Lives* we see more concretely why the ancients saw in pleasure a threat to community. In addition, we begin to understand how public men could use their consciousness of this potential spur to divided loyalties as a weapon in the competition over standing and allegiance. Plutarch represents the tension between public duty and private pleasure as an area in which all political men routinely faced accusations levied by rivals. Writing as a historian, Plutarch himself hands on these accusations when he wishes to encourage the reader's suspicion of a man's character, and deflects them when he wants the reader to believe in the man's good faith and fitness for public office. In the *Life of Pompey* Plutarch is on the defensive. He reports the charges of sexual excess made against the man, but attempts to dismiss them as unjustified accusations invented by Pompey's enemies. In the *Life of*

Antony, however, it is Plutarch himself who accuses his subject of dissolution brought on by unchecked lust and a woman's charm. Given the centrality of Pompey and Antony as military opponents of Julius Caesar and Octavian, it is clear that Plutarch perceived these private matters as bearing on the most significant of public events, the Roman transition from republic to empire.

The *Life of Pompey* paints its hero as constantly troubled by charges of immoderation from his political oppononents, but it adduces the charges in a random manner, as if to suggest that the annoyance was nothing more than a routine hazard of public life. The implication, of course, is that the accusations were unfounded: despite Pompey's numerous marriages, we are assured that he was not particularly susceptible to feminine charms. Plutarch reports that Pompey was beloved for his *sōphrosynē,* and that no Roman ever enjoyed such well-deserved good will from his compatriots (1.4). Early in the *Life* we encounter Pompey taking care to protect his reputation from groundless slurs by especially circumspect conduct. But the effort is in vain: "still he could not escape the censures of his enemies: he was accused of neglecting and betraying many public interests on account of married women."[14]

If we pay closer attention, however, we see that Plutarch is being disingenuous, for many of the accusations levied at Pompey took their origin in his political marriages. His repudiation of Antistia and marriage to Aemilia in order to strengthen his political alliance with Sulla (newly proclaimed dictator)[15] elicit defensive explanation: "This marriage was the act of a tyrant, and befitted the needs of Sulla rather than the nature and habits of Pompey" (9.3). What elicited the criticism may have been the seeming insincerity of the short-lived matches or the tendency of repeated honeymoons to distract the statesman from his responsibilities. To be appraised as abetting the social order, a marriage (whether pleasureless or passionate) had to be seen as establishing a lasting social contract between families.

We can see in the case of Pompey's marriage to Julia, the daughter of Julius Caesar, the multiple lines of attack against a marriage that did not establish a solid dynastic allegiance. As he narrates a scene of battle between Pompey and Caesar after Julia's death, Plutarch summarizes the comments of Pompey's critics: "the family alliance which had been made [between the two men], and the charms of Julia, along with the marriage, were now seen to have been from the first the deceitful and suspect pledges of a partnership based in self-interest; there was no real friendship [between Pompey and Caesar] in it" (70.7). Affection between spouses was not enough to protect the men contracting the match from this kind of criticism.

Indeed, conjugal feeling was not necessarily a social good; it was only perceived in that light where it induced the spouses toward responsible behavior in their relationships outside the marriage. Plutarch reports that Pompey's marriage to Julia was seen as immoderately affectionate:

> he incurred . . . jealous ill-will *(phthonon)* because, handing over his provinces and his armies to legates who were his old friends, he himself went about in Italy from one pleasure-spot to another, keeping company with his wife, either because he loved her, or because she loved him so that he could not bear to leave her. (53.1)

Similarly, Plutarch records criticism of Pompey as he celebrates another marriage, this time to Cornelia, criticism in which the nuptial merriment is explicitly linked to an abandonment of his more sober duty toward the city of Rome (55.4–5). But Plutarch does not choose to specify Pompey himself as responsible for the political vulnerability caused by his irregular married life. A faithful and affectionate marriage of long standing would have served as a shield against the insinuations to which all political men were exposed, as Plutarch well knew, but to side with Pompey's accusers even to the degree of holding him responsible for the instability of his married life would undermine the broader reading of the man.

In the *Life of Antony,* however, Plutarch himself stands as the accuser. His treatment of Antony's politically disastrous attachment to the Ptolemaic queen of Egypt, Cleopatra VII, is a case study in the addiction by which a man subverts his political and military obligations, succumbing to the whims of the woman by whom he is bewitched. Antony's intemperate and self-destructive behavior is shown to have had repercussions not only for his public standing but for the Roman state itself.

Antony is already romantically entangled with Cleopatra, and already in an unsteady relationship with his political ally and rival Octavian, when a marriage alliance is proposed between the two men through Octavian's sister Octavia. All parties are aware that the tension between Antony and Octavian poses the risk of civil war, and with hindsight the reader knows that it will lead to the end of the Roman republic. When the idea of the marriage is introduced, Plutarch adduces the Roman people's view of Octavia as a woman capable of bringing order and moderation not only to Antony's personal life but to the Roman state:

> Everybody tried to bring about this marriage. They hoped that Octavia—having, besides her great beauty, intelligence and dignity—would be so beloved by Antony (as such a woman must be) when they were married that she would be able to restore [political] harmony and salvage the situation entirely. (31.4)

That the marriage was not a success is of course well known to Plutarch's intended reader, and the inevitable result of Antony's subsequent insult to Octavia—and through her to Octavian—by his continued preference for Cleopatra over the legitimate Roman bride is thus foreshadowed.

Plutarch dramatizes Antony's downfall by casting it in the midst of the life-or-death contingencies of civil war. The decisive moment occurs in Antony's preposterous handling of the battle of Actium. In this memorable scene, Antony first chooses to fight the battle at sea in order to please Cleopatra—despite his far superior power on land—and then betrays his men by chasing after Cleopatra when she flees the scene:

> Here, Antony made it clear to all the world that he was following neither the sentiments of a commander nor those of a brave man, nor even of his own: as someone said in pleasantry that the soul of a lover dwells in another's body, he was drawn along by the woman as if he had become incorporate with her and must go where she did. (66.7)

It did not seem incidental to Plutarch that Antony's passion resulted in the squandering of human life, and of the Roman republic itself.

We will encounter these four figures—the public man and his rival for power, the legitimate wife and the adulterous temptress—over and over again in the literature of the Roman empire. That the marriage between Octavia and Antony was not successful in producing the desired social stability serves as a warning that womanly influence was less a matter of the real historical effect that women exerted on their husbands and lovers than of an interpretive pattern, a sort of narrative shorthand that could be used to account for and even to influence a man's success or failure in the bid for power.

The drama of Cleopatra's destructive allure is heightened by its antithesis to Octavia's restorative moderation. In both cases, the female character's narrative function was to call attention to the issue of the man's self-control and loyalty to his allies and to the common good. In narrative terms, a man's illicit lover was expected to draw him away from duty and toward the pursuit of private interests, while his legitimate wife was expected to deploy the same womanly influence to a purpose altogether more sober. What both figures have in common is their persuasiveness.

Thus we see in the *Lives* a motive for Plutarch's proposal in the *Erōtikos* of marriage as friendship. In the philosophical writings, marriage is presented as an institution particularly able to foster moderation and stability in the participants—and thus the common good—because of its ability to harness the power of desire. Aphrodite collaborates in "the unity . . . that Eros creates when he undertakes a partnership in marriage" (769F), sealing with the consummation of pleasure a unity more sound than another kind of friendship could forge. But what is really at stake is not desire per se but masculine character and reliability. The *Lives* warn of the political weakness from which a man could suffer if it were believed that his private life might sway him from his public duty, emphasizing the disaster to which such indulgence could lead for those foolish or weak enough to court it. We learn from the *Lives* that when women and their influence are discussed, their appearance should be read as a sign that a man's character is in question, whether its virtue is to be defended or its dissolution illustrated.

Male Competition, Female Experience

The image of women influencing men served as the basis of a persuasive moral language for a number of reasons. Its magnetism was linked partly to narrative economy: by metonymy, sexual temperance was understood vividly and memorably to index the self-control of a male protagonist in matters other than the sexual. Its power came also from a modest reenactment of the practice it was marking: the vicarious pleasure that its appearance presumably afforded a male reader. Finally, it was venerable. From the garden of Eden to the judgment of Paris, the founding literatures of the ancient Mediterranean had used the topos of womanly influence to amplify the tension between a man's private interests and his loyalty to those who might place their trust in him.[16]

For a man to perceive the interdependence of his own good with that of the larger community required substantial self-mastery, since in the handling of financial, political, and military obligations there were often occasions where his immediate interests might seem to be served by unscrupulous dealings. It was important to create a powerful moral language, both to deter men from the temptation to betray the common good and to use as a weapon against men who had done so. In his *City of God*, Augustine of Hippo would remember the virtuous *maiores* in language which made clear this connection between sexual intemperance and the civic vices:

> They took no account of their own material interest compared with the common good, that is the commonwealth and the public purse; they resisted the temptations of avarice; they acted for their country's well-being with disinterested concern; they were guilty of no offence against the law; they succumbed to no sensual indulgence.[17]

The temptation to sensual indulgence, and the power of the sexually tempting to sway the judgment of those under their spell, served as a potent narrative emblem of the unpredictable factor of private interest in the actions of public men.

A man's ability manifestly to dissociate himself from the weaknesses which made for social instability was a critical element in his claim to honor, a claim which needed constantly to be justified, both within the brotherhood of aristocratic men and in the larger arena of a society in which these were by definition a minority. Reported performance (whether of private austerities or of public benefactions) was the coin by which honor was purchased, yet the sphere of the private bore particular semiotic importance. This meant that the public man had continuously to project his trustworthiness before a public eye well trained in discerning signs of weakness in body, mind, or will. The situation was not unlike what John Winkler, quoting Xenophon, describes for classical Athens:

> At all levels of practical morality and advice-giving we find the undisciplined person described as someone mastered or conquered by something over which he should exert control . . . Whether choosing

a general to save the city (Xen. *Mem.* 1.5.1) or a bailiff to manage the farm (Xen. *Econ.* 12.13), one wants a man who is the honorable master of his pleasures, not—by the logic of zero-sum competition—the shameful slave of them (*tais hēdonais douleuōn aischrōs*, Xen. *Mem.* 1.5.5).[18]

A man could expect his always numerous enemies to seize any opportunity to represent him as a bad bet in the perennially renegotiated network of allegiances and interdependencies. While his standing was subject to the flux of ascendancy between his supporters and his detractors, it was in his interest to give the detractors as little as possible to work with.

If a man's enemies were bent on discerning in his private life an intemperance that could compromise the fulfillment of public duty, it was his task to undermine the plausibility of such revelations by a deft broadcasting of his probity. This meant that he should make as public as possible his solemn affection for the chaste women of his family. Paradoxically, the modesty of his wife and female relatives was of use to him only if it was widely acknowledged. Thus it would emerge as a critical element in the ceaseless struggle over a man's, and a family's, reputation.

This consciousness of public scrutiny meant that cultivating a facade of exemplary temperance was approached as a long-term commitment, to be maintained over generations. The public gestures of a Roman household—including well-publicized "private" behavior and attitudes—would have been understood, by both the actors and their audience, as a compilation of rhetorical resources on behalf of the family's claim to power. It follows that the Roman rhetoric of marital concord is open to misapprehension by readers whose awareness of honor and reputation as prerequisite to vital allegiances is no longer keen.

If what is argued here is true, there are dramatic implications for our understanding of ancient women's history and experience. On one hand, it undermines our already scarce source material. If we allow that many ancient accounts of female behavior are shaped rhetorically to suit a judgment of male character, this means that their reflection of reality is distorted. On the other hand, to concentrate on these distortions will afford a more accurate picture of how ancient women understood themselves.

It is particularly difficult for English-speaking scholars to assess the experience of ancient men and women without reference to a post-Enlightenment conception of individual autonomy. This makes it difficult to capture the importance of women's agency within and on behalf of the household. The assumption tends to be that since their position was in general structurally lower than that of similarly ranked men (unless other factors, such as privileged access to a more powerful family system through the married woman's parents, disrupted the gendered ordering), both they and their male counterparts would have considered their actions in the private sphere to have minor significance compared to men's more noteworthy activity in public. Such a view is of course anachronistic: the notion of a "private" sphere divested of "public" significance would have seemed impossible (and undesirable) to the ancient mind. The *domus,* along with its aspects of family and dynasty, was the primary unit of cultural identity, political significance, and economic production.

All of this means that aristocratic women saw their highly visible "invisibility" within the domestic sphere as a source of power and identity. It was not necessarily incompatible with direct intervention beyond the walls of the *domus:* the substantial civic patronage that women exerted in their own name was understood as reinforcing, rather than undermining, the ideology of domestic concord.[19] When we come to the problem of how women were affected by changes in the representation of conjugal affect, we shall see that Roman married women of the upper classes jealously guarded their prominent symbolic function within the rhetoric of womanly influence, and fiercely resented the introduction of an alternate moral language that challenged their symbolic position as arbiters of masculine virtue.

To cast light on the dynamics of identity and status negotiation, it may be useful to borrow from contemporary linguistic theory. A variety of subdisciplines within linguistics have emerged over the last half-century in response to J. L. Austin's 1955 lectures on speech-act theory, which outlined the conditions under which speech constitutes (or fosters) the reality it claims to describe, and Erving Goffman's analysis of "face" (which focuses on the self as social performance) and "frame" (which focuses on the way a given presentation of conversational material calls attention to the terms of the relationship between speaker and hearer).[20] Interactional sociolinguistics and cognate methods under the broad category of discourse analysis draw on sociology and anthropology as much as on linguistics or the philosophy of language.[21]

Bronwyn Davies and Rom Harré have recently argued that in addition to describing or confirming relationships and roles, speech is the medium through which the terms of relationships and thus the contours of the self are negotiated, not only explicitly but through a continuous dialectic of experimental self-assertion structured into the way language is used. The force of this negotiation may be cumulative—that is, the past discursive practice of a speaker can influence how listeners hear what is said—but the speaker cannot dictate the listener's interpretation. This leads to interdependence among speakers and to the volatility of the speech medium. According to this model, the intent of the speaker does not govern the effective content of speech:

> Are we to think of conversation as a hazardous de-coding (by the hearers) of the individual social intentions of each speaker? Searle's (1979) version of Austin's (1975) speech act theory of conversation certainly tends in that direction, since he takes the type of a speech act to be defined by the social intention of the person who uttered it. We will argue here that, on the contrary, a conversation unfolds through the joint action of all the participants as they make (or attempt to make) their own and each other's actions socially determinate . . . what it is that has been said evolves and changes as the conversation develops.[22]

Similarly, what one refers to as a speaker's "identity" is drawn from the fluid medium of speech encounters rather than from the speaker's initial intention.

This is significant in that the speaker is in some sense dependent on his or her interlocutors not only for allegiance or affirmation but for the structuring of his or her very sense of self:

> An individual emerges through the processes of social interaction, not as a relatively fixed end product but as one who is constituted and reconstituted through the various discursive practices in which they participate. Accordingly, who one is is always an open question with a shifting answer depending upon the positions made available within one's own and others' discursive practices. (46)

This means that as speakers are positioning themselves and others, they are simultaneously being positioned. While speakers may intend their speech to be understood according to a certain interpretive scheme, they must also allow for "the availability of alternative discourses to the one invoked by the initial speaker (and particularly of discourses which offer a critique to the one invoked by the initial speaker)" (49). Where speech encounters are understood as competitive, or where they serve to negotiate status, the problem of conflicting interpretive schemes has far-reaching consequences.

Sociolinguists have only recently learned to appreciate the fragmentary, ad hoc, and incomplete nature of the process by which speech encounters determine identity. This has depended on the rise of a post-structuralist sensibility and an immanentist view of language, in which speech acts are seen not as the incidental expression of a transcendental syntax but rather as discrete attempts to propose meaning. Meaning is only achieved progressively: how a speech act should be understood is determined through discourse, that is, through its perceived relation to other known speech acts. Interpretation is intersubjective, cumulative, and each new speech act is as important as the last one to a hearer's (or a speaker's) perception of prevailing discursive practice.

Such a theory is particularly useful for understanding a society that placed enormous importance on reputation negotiated through public speech.[23] One might trace, say, the use of the rhetorical topos of sexual immoderation as a tool by which an orator could position himself as the man of reason standing against the outrages of a madman. To return to the case of Antony, such an approach would set aside Plutarch and take up instead the Cicero of the *Second Philippic*, where the attempt to undermine the progress of a self-proclaimed dictator takes the form of a crossreferencing of the man's political and sexual excesses, framed as a speech to be given in the Senate. (The speech was eventually circulated in written rather than spoken form; Cicero's murder some months later at the hands of Antony's officers may explain the precaution.) This kind of approach to the texts cited by Veyne, for example, would be a worthwhile study in itself.

Our task, however, is somewhat more complicated. Rather than charting the use of the rhetoric of *sōphrosynē* and womanly influence on one or even more than one occasion, the intent here is to chart the subversion of the rhetorical economy itself and to extend the insights of sociolinguistic positioning from individuals to cultural communities. We will see how a group claims the allegiance of new members by indicating that its leadership is morally superior. But we will also see that in the historical or parahistorical treatment of male heroic figures and their female counterparts, the moral language of *sōphrosynē* could be diverted from maintaining the claims of the city and the common good to challenging the right of either city or household to make claims on the individual.

Narrative Invention and the Rhetoric of Gender

It was Christian writers who subverted the moral language of *sōphrosynē*, but it would be a mistake to suggest a monolithic Christian rejection of marital concord, self-mastery, or the good influence of women. To the contrary, the silent majority of Christians would have stood as traditionalists on this matter, and even those writers responsible for the rhetorical subversion might well have been shocked by its consequences.

To understand how the memory of a hero could be reshaped according to the traditional rhetoric of womanly influence, there is no better example than the story of the fall of John Chrysostom, bishop of Constantinople at the turn of the fifth century. The circumstances of John's downfall are obscure, but not for lack of documentation. In fact, a variety of nearly contemporaneous sources provide a variety of evidence, much of it conflicting. It is through this rich layering of narratives pertaining to an event in the life of an otherwise well-documented individual that we gain a rare opportunity to chart a legend in the making.

In the recounting, John's unparalleled prowess as a Christian preacher and his recorded preference for modesty in women were developed into a full-blown historical drama, centered on the pernicious influence of the empress Eudoxia on her husband and her use of that influence to destroy John. Since all of the versions include the detail of an altercation between the bishop and the empress as the turning point in his downfall, but none agree about the nature of the altercation, it is clear that the empress' place in the narrative cannot be explained by historical fact.

Drawing on his study of what seems to have been the earliest account of John's downfall, a eulogy preserved in the manuscripts as the *Life of Chrysostom* by Martyrius of Antioch, Florent van Ommeslaeghe has traced the emergence of the tendency to explain John's ruin by an encounter with Eudoxia.[24] The beginnings of this process of accretion are deceptively slight. Soon after John's death, his biographer, Palladius of Helenopolis, recorded a charge of treason among the imputations against John, which his enemies at the Synod of the Oak collected and forwarded to the emperor Arcadius. Palladius explains that the treasonous act imputed to John was a slur against the empress Eudoxia comparing her to the biblical queen Jezebel.[25] Palladius does not suggest that John had in fact so spoken, but attempts to account for the circumstances in which a false charge might have been plotted.[26]

What emerges from van Ommeslaeghe's study is that none of the early accounts of John's downfall included reliable information about the encounter with Eudoxia. For example, Martyrius' account, which must have been pronounced or circulated immediately after Chrysostom's death (and thus predates Palladius), shares with later narrations the element of John's clash with Eudoxia, but in an entirely different form. The later accounts build on the charge recorded by Palladius, that John had compared Eudoxia to Jezebel, with each writer attempting to supply a context for John's having made the comparison. Eventually this process resulted in an elaborate set piece built around John, Eudoxia, and a Constantinopolitan vineyard, a narrative inspired by the episode of Jezebel and Naboth's vineyard in 1 Kings 21.1–16.

Martyrius, however, knew a different version of the trouble between John and Eudoxia. He remembered the empress suggesting that John should abdicate his bishop See, reassuring him that she would bear the responsibility before God of John's having abandoned his call. His response is recorded: "Truly, madam, I doubt you would be able to serve as my guarantor; it was of no use to Adam to say that he had been seduced by Eve, nor to Eve to hide behind the serpent. Rather, God punished each for his (or her) own sin."[27] According to Martyrius, the empress saw in this a likening of herself to Eve and, by extension, a treasonous charge against the emperor himself.

A variety of comparable accounts of John's fall subsequently arose. Each writer, among them not only preachers but learned historians, supplemented the story of John's accusation against Eudoxia by scripting his actual speech, usually embellished with allusions to Old or New Testament female treachery. Some later narratives attempted to reconcile the version given by Martyrius to that of Palladius; in one case, Eudoxia is figured simultaneously as Jezebel, Eve, and Herodias.[28]

These encrustations had a logic of their own. John's accusers at the Synod of the Oak had intended to represent him as a danger to the state. If he had slandered Eudoxia, he could be represented not only as treasonous but as given to the kind of excess excited in men by women, even if in this case the intemperance took the form of anger (as opposed to lust, the more customary charge).[29] But by harnessing the memorable detail of an (unspecified) clash with Eudoxia to their own narrative purposes, John's later champions could invert the force of the suggestion of womanly influence, defending him against intemperance and commuting the remembered charge into a heroic effort to further the common good. What all parties sensed was the narrative power of the episode.

The case admirably illustrates how readily historical traditions attach colorful if misleading detail to the compelling element of a heroic man's encounter with a woman, especially where the man's character, and hence the acceptance or rejection of what he stands for, hangs in the balance. If we assume for the sake of argument that wherever a woman is mentioned a man's character is being judged—and along with it what he stands for—we can begin to see the rhetorical possibilities afforded by a female point of identification in a literature aimed at defending, or undermining, such sanctified Greco-Roman institutions as marriage, the family, and even the city itself. This helps to account for a much-discussed feature of ancient writings that have come down to us without explicit context or authorial intent: their striking emphasis on female protagonists. We will see that attention to the rhetorical function of the heroine in two groups of texts—the ancient Greek novel and the Apocryphal Acts of the Apostles—will shed new light on the relation between the two genres. Similarly we will be able to understand how the civic ideology of marriage, which had served for at least a millennium as a symbolic reinforcement of social stability, lost ground to a model of otherworldly allegiance and a corresponding ideal of Christian virginity.

· 2 ·

The Ancient Novel

"When I was hunting in Lesbos, I saw the most beautiful sight I have ever seen, in a grove that was sacred to the Nymphs: a painting that told a story of love . . . women giving birth, others dressing the babies, babies exposed, animals suckling them, shepherds adopting them, young people pledging love, a pirates' raid, an enemy attack—and more, much more, all of it romantic. I gazed in admiration and was seized by a yearning to depict the picture in words.

"I searched out an interpreter of the picture and produced the four volumes of this book, as an offering to Love (erōs), the Nymphs, and Pan, and something for mankind to possess and enjoy. It will cure the sick, comfort the distressed, stir the memory of those who have loved, and educate those who haven't. For certainly no one has ever avoided Love, and no one will, as long as beauty exists, and eyes can see. As for me—may the god Love let me write about others' passions but keep my own self-control."[1]

A squire at hunt, happening on a shrine to the Nymphs and charmed by its decoration, seeks out a local cicerone to tell its history. The guide in turn proves competent to draw forth from the shrine's frescoed scenes a full-blown pastoral: a goatherd and a shepherdess fell in love, and their hopes of marriage were thwarted until their high birth was revealed and their marriage feast could be celebrated at the shrine. Thus opens Longus of Mytilene's second-century romance of Daphnis and Chloe.

If we restore two key Greek words to the final line of the proem as translated above—"may the god *Erōs* let me write about others' passions but keep my own *sōphrosynē*"—we can see that Longus opens up an intriguing perspective on the problem of how ancient fiction reflected, or helped to shape, views of marriage. What did it mean for a writer to offer himself as a model of comic, reluctant self-control, one inclined to relate with relish the passions of others? More than one scholar has argued that the novel, with its ironic eroticism and its quasi-philosophical emphasis on the marriage of hero and heroine as a partnership, constitutes an important source for the social and intellectual history of sexuality in the Roman period.[2] It has also been noted that detailed description of the nubile heroine in various rituals of sexual foreplay establishes a bond of complicity between the (presumably male) author and the intended reader (also presumably male), through the reader's identification with the hero's desire for the heroine.[3] In this chapter I will argue that the ancient romance was designed to mobilize this complicity in desire on behalf of the social order.

Let us begin with five Greek novels, the surviving texts that constitute the canon known collectively as the ancient romance. They were produced between the first century BCE and the sixth century CE by five more or less distinguished writers: Chariton, *Chaereas and Callirhoe*; Xenophon of Ephesus, *An Ephesian Tale*; Achilles Tatius, *Leukippe and Kleitophon*; Longus, *Daphnis and Chloe*; and Heliodorus, *An Ethiopian Story*. The genre has been characterized succinctly by B. P. Reardon, whose edited volume of English translations of these and related texts has led to an explosion of interest in it:

> Hero and heroine are always young, wellborn, and handsome; their marriage is disrupted or prevented by separation, travel in distant parts, and a series of misfortunes, usually spectacular. Virginity or chastity, at least in the female, is of crucial importance, and fidelity to one's partner, together often with trust in the gods, will ultimately guarantee a happy ending.[4]

Love and adventure, displacement and danger: the elements of romance are shared with other genres, but the mixture is recognizable.

Our understanding of these stories is vexed by fragmentary information on such fundamentals as date and audience, in part because for whatever reason the genre did not attract the attention of ancient literary critics. The modern scholarly discussion starts from Erwin Rohde's pronouncement in 1876 that the texts were produced at the end of the Roman period, with their generic anomaly a witness to the period's cultural inadequacy. Subsequent attempts to rehabilitate the romance as something more than subliterary hack work have challenged both the late date—papyrus fragments suggest that the genre existed as early as the Hellenistic period—and the insinuation that their authors were incompetent.[5]

At issue in the discussion of dating and literary level of the genre has been its relationship to ancient religion, whether the religious traditions the texts themselves describe[6] or the parallel texts that take a more explicit interest in religious affiliation, the Jewish *Joseph and Aseneth* and the Christian Apocryphal Acts of the Apostles. Ben Edwin Perry, who did much to encourage appreciation of the romances' literary merit, buttressed his claims by the argument that they were early and by deft use of the "Christian romances, so-called" as a foil to their merit. He classified the pagan texts as both infinitely superior and decidedly secular.[7] That the study of the ancient romance has yet to be informed by attention to its Jewish or Christian counterparts is a result of Perry's equation of the secular with the culturally superior. A counterproductive disciplinary line has been drawn between the study of "religious" (Jewish or Christian) and "secular" (pagan) literature in antiquity. This kind of stereotyping by religious affiliation is misleading, whatever its attractiveness to the kind of classicist who establishes the sophistication of a genre by distancing it from those literary parallels presumed to emanate from an anti-intellectual population of religious fanatics, or to the kind of theologian who wants to claim a pristine divine inspiration, unmediated by secular culture, for any authentic religious voice.[8] It will become clear in what follows that neither genre can be fully understood without reference to the other.

In the absence of external evidence about who wrote or read them and why,[9] the social location of the romances has had to be deduced from the texts themselves. Because of their interest in love and adventure, they were seen until recently by scholars as frivolous, anti-intellectual, or both. If cultural decadence was discounted as an explanation for the romances' imputed literary failings, the next best theory was that the intended readership was female. But this view is no longer accepted,[10] and the concentration of interest in themes of love and marriage requires a less dismissive explanation. A good starting point is that the romances are intellectual and frivolous at the same time, a literature of intentional playfulness directed to an audience of literate men.[11] Following this line of reasoning, Simon Goldhill invites us to account for the narrative interest of the love theme by reconsidering the intersection of pleasure and text in the ancient literature on desire.[12] But the "serious" purpose of the romances—and their emphasis on the charms of love and a nubile heroine—has yet to be identified.

Since we know so little about the concerns and commitments of those who produced the romances, there is the danger of assuming too quickly that the elements of comedy, frivolity, and charm were offered to the reader purely as entertainment. But romance, we will see, spoke in a voice both light-hearted and acutely serious to the men and women of the ancient polis. Whatever resolution is offered to the problem of dating the genre's rise, whether it emerges in the Hellenistic period or under Roman dominion, its interest in the love problems of adolescents provides an important clue to the concerns of the regional aristocracies that maintained in flesh and stone the infrastructure of a Mediterranean-wide empire.

One runs a risk, perhaps, by invoking so well-worn an idea as romance. The problem is exacerbated in English, where the terms "romance" and "novel" carry distracting connotations. It should be stated at the outset that "romance" is not meant here with the high seriousness of Northrop Frye and his literary descendants or with the medieval specificity of Eugène Vinaver and his. But still the ancient texts that have been known in English as the ancient or Hellenistic romance do have something in common—the way in which the relationship of reader and text, reader and author, is figured in the marital schemings of noble-spirited adolescents. If romance was at one level about persuasion—about a writer romancing a reader—the cultural historian is bound to ask, who was being persuaded to do what?

The complicity of desire in romance would have enlisted the male reader in the renewal of the social order both symbolically, through the ideology of marriage as "a rampart for the city,"[13] and practically, by encouraging the generation of legitimate offspring. Attention in my next chapter to the romance's closest "sibling" genre in antiquity, the Christian Apocryphal Acts, will show that our most significant evidence for the romance's ancient readers suggests that they saw it as carrying precisely this kind of civic message.

By situating romance in the broader context of the place of *erōs* in the Greek literature of the Roman empire, I will argue that irony and desire functioned together to mediate an important aspect of Roman social relations: the dynastic concerns of the provincial aristocracies. We see here a harnessing of desire—the hero's desire and the reader's desire—to a moral: at the tale's end, the marriage feast must be celebrated, and the work of maintaining and renewing the city must begin.

Romance and the Pleasures

The romance, it goes without saying, was not the only literary genre to experiment with desire and pleasure. We see in the Roman period a continuing interest in the problem of desire as it had been set out in the *Symposium*. With one telling exception, these inheritors of Plato dispense with what they perceive as his hypocritical, self-justificatory moralizing on hypothetical types of pleasure,[14] and accept pleasure— celebrate it—as a social fact. But we will see that even there the ancient romance steers close to Plutarch's position that the power of desire can be turned, through marriage, to the common good.

Four literary restagings of the *Symposium* debate survive from antiquity, one an episode from Achilles Tatius's *Leukippe and Kleitophon*. The first, Plutarch's *Erōtikos*, written at the turn of the second century, we have already seen. There Plato's rather solemn debate, which justifies desire—particularly homosexual desire—by means of a pursuit of the Beautiful through contemplation of the beloved, finds an ironic reversal. Since even the philosopher is prone to the constraints of *erōs*, Plutarch suggests that true *sōphrosynē* is achieved only by the man who takes pleasure as a given and condemns not pleasure itself but excess, abuse, and hypocrisy, which, designed to conceal these vices, is the most reprehensible vice of all.

Although Plutarch's willingness to attach a positive moral value to marriage as a chaste, harmonious outlet for a man's susceptibility to desire does influence the romance, it was his ironic stance toward the debate on pleasure which united his literary heirs. They viewed the debate as something between otiose speculation and rank hypocrisy. Closest to Plutarch in form there is the *Erōtes* of Pseudo-Lucian, which takes it up from an intentionally absurdist perspective.[15]

Here the setting of the debate is ironic to the point of ridicule. What for Plato had been a serious inquiry into the powers of Eros and Aphrodite becomes a tourist excursion to Aphrodite's temple at Cnidos. Picking up on Plato's assertion that pederasty is more appropriate to the pursuit of virtue than desire for women, the Athenian Kallikratidas and the Corinthian Charikles argue whether the front or the back of the statue is more sexually arousing.[16] After a temple attendant weighs in with the tale of a previous visitor who did indeed spend a night of passion with the statue (a stain on Aphrodite's inner thigh is given as proof), the men agree to debate the question in earnest. Lykinos, a witness to the debate, is charged with acting as judge, and it is his account, retold to a third friend, Theomnestos, that we hear. After recounting the debate, Lykinos confesses to finding the Athenian's argument in favor of pederasty more compelling, and his friend Theomnestos initially accepts the judgment as valid. Eventually, though, Theomnestos begins unwittingly to echo the criticisms that the Corinthian, arguing in favor of marriage, has made against the Athenian.

Charikles insinuates that the philosophical argument in favor of pederasty is hypocritical. If adoration of the beloved is meant to aid in the pursuit of virtue, why then would a man like Socrates choose to love a physically attractive and morally ambivalent boy rather than a withered but eminently virtuous old man? This is how he puts it:

Of course the followers of Socrates can always trot out a dazzling line of reasoning—by which childish ears inexperienced in logic are tricked even if one who has already arrived at sufficient reason would not be swayed. For they feign a love for the soul and—ashamed of paying court to the beauty of the body—call themselves lovers of virtue. This makes me laugh aloud! Grave philosophers, what has happened to you? You dismiss with scorn what through time has shown its quality by the evidence of old age and grey hairs, while all your wise desire is excited by the new, which does not as yet have within it the reasoning to judge between right and wrong. (23)

When Lykinos' listener, Theomnestos, is asked to comment on the debate, he takes up the same argument from the opposite direction:

I marvelled very much at the solemnity of the austere arguments on behalf of pederasty, only I did not think it very delightful to spend the day with a youth enduring the punishment of Tantalos, and—with beauty washing my eyes with its waves—to submit to thirst instead of drawing water. (53)

In his case, what we have is a criticism of the high-minded defense of pederasty from the perspective not of the defender of marriage but rather of the pederast who prefers his pleasures untrammeled by any pretense of modesty. Theomnestos goes on to offer his own clear idea of how a boy should be seduced:

May it fall to me to love boys in this way! But let the heavenly-minded and the philosophically high-brow beguile the unlearned with ingenious inventions of solemn names—if anyone was dedicated to desire Socrates was, and having laid down with him beneath a single womanish cape Alcibiades did not arise untouched. (54)

By alluding to Plato's claim that the affair between Socrates and Alcibiades was never consummated, not only does Theomnestos ridicule the hypocrisy of the Athenian Kallikratidas, but Pseudo-Lucian ridicules the whole tradition of defense of pederasty stretching back to Plato. His point, however, is not to condemn pederasty. Pseudo-Lucian is writing in the comic vein, and it is his business to celebrate desire.

A similarly affectionate disrespect for high-mindedness obtains in the ancient romances. Achilles Tatius' *Leukippe and Kleitophon* reinvents the *Symposium* in a fondly ridiculous version. Kleitophon and Leukippe elope and board a ship to Alexandria; during the journey, a shipboard friendship springs up between Kleitophon and an Egyptian, Menelaos, who mourns the death of his male lover three years before. Seeking to distract Menelaos from his grief, Kleitophon challenges him to a reenactment of the familiar debate whether women or boys are more desirable as lovers.[17] The consolation is successful, and the two men become firm friends.

It is clearly the author's intention that this unusual episode of male bonding should arouse his reader's interest in the long-deferred wedding night of Kleitophon and Leukippe; high philosophical discourse is knowingly reduced to the level of an author's teasing of his reader. The irony is that the reader is not in the end admitted to the bridal chamber itself: Achilles Tatius dispenses with the "long-awaited marriage" in a single clause of his final chapter (8.19). When we hear the sexually inexperienced Kleitophon championing a hypothetical female lover's "passionate kisses within kisses" to the more experienced Menelaos, the irony is in part that what Kleitophon delights in talking about, not yet having experienced it, and what the reader delights in hearing about, is something the reader will no longer be privy to once Kleitophon attains the object of his desire. The salacious is yoked here to an idea of conjugal virtue not far from Plutarch's.

The other Greek romances share both the coy and the salacious aspects of Achilles Tatius' narrative. Although the details vary, each of the romances has at its core the romantic education of a young couple who must overcome a variety of obstacles to marital union, and each narrative dwells with relish on the details of their sexual misadventures. The reader is understood to share in the couple's ardent expectation of the much-deferred consummation of their legitimate marriage: titillation and social responsibility join forces in the reader's craving for detail and the author's willingness to provide it. Love, here, is not in tension with the social order: rather, the celebration of desire is a celebration of the social order's replenishment.

By contrast, we should remember one final rewriting of Plato's *Symposium*, the *Symposium, or Dialogue on Virginity* of Methodius, bishop of Olympos at the turn of the fourth century. Delighting in an opportunity to brandish both erudition and religious zeal, Methodius alters the terms of the Platonic debate almost—but not quite—beyond recognition. Instead of an argument on pleasure and the philosophical life, as in Plato, or on the virtues of love for boys and love for women, as in Plutarch and his successors, Methodius stages a dialogue among unmarried women, who debate whether a virgin's claim to self-control is superior if she experiences no sexual desire whatever, or if she does experience sexual desire and perseveres in abstaining from its consummation.

Plutarch, Pseudo-Lucian, and Achilles Tatius all take for granted a degree of sexual license for the man of virtue; the question is how his sexual activity should be inflected. Methodius alters the basic assumption in two distinct ways. First, he removes the supposition of sexual activity and replaces it with abstinence. Second, he alters the gender of the interlocutors: the shift is from a company of sexually active males to one of virginal females. We will see in the next chapter how the ideal of sexual continence and the figure of the continent heroine served the apologetic purposes of early Christian literature. Our immediate task is to understand what message the ideal of conjugal love and the figure of the desired and desiring bride in the romance were designed to convey to the ancient reader.

Love and Marriage

The earliest of the surviving romances, *Chaereas and Callirhoe,* makes it clear from the outset that the desire of the hero and heroine has a public dimension and a civic purpose. The two great statesmen of Syracuse, the general Hermocrates, "the man who defeated the Athenians," and Ariston, "second only to Hermocrates in Syracuse," each have a child, Hermocrates a girl and Ariston a boy. "The two were political rivals, so that they would have made a marriage alliance with anyone rather than with each other. But Eros likes to win and enjoys succeeding against the odds."[18]

The chance meeting of the star-crossed lovers is staged against a backdrop of great civic institutions, rendered in a two-dimensional, almost tongue-in-cheek style. Still the peculiar intimacy of their first encounter is all the more vivid in the telling because of the contrast:

A public festival of Aphrodite took place, and almost all the women went to her temple. Callirhoe had never been out in public before, but her father wanted her to do reverence to the goddess, and her mother took her. Just at that time Chaereas was walking home from the gymnasium; he was radiant as a star, the flush of exercise blooming on his bright countenance like gold on silver. Now, chance would have it that at the corner of a narrow street the two walked straight into each other; the god had contrived the meeting so they would see each other. At once, they were both smitten with love . . . beauty had met nobility. (1.1)

It is in fact the public aspect of their romance that saves the couple initially, for when Chaereas begins to waste away for love of Callirhoe his father refuses to approach Hermocrates to propose the marriage. But the will of the people is for the young couple to be joined.

> The gymnasium missed Chaereas; it was almost deserted, for he was the idol of the young folk. They asked after him, and when they found out what had made him ill, they all felt pity for a handsome youth who looked as if he would die because his noble heart was broken. A regular assembly took place at this time. When the people had taken their seats, their first and only cry was: "Noble Hermocrates, great general, save Chaereas! That will be your finest monument! The city pleads for the marriage, today, of a pair worthy of each other!" Who could describe that assembly? It was dominated by Eros. Hermocrates loved his country and could not refuse what it asked. (1.1)

Thus Hermocrates renounces the rivalry with Ariston as a gesture of civic piety. The tone here is comic melodrama, but the point is a serious one. Competition among families might be in the interest of the competitors, but the interest of the wider community was served by cooperation.

Similarly, the resolution of the narrative is framed in terms of the young couple's triumphant return to their city at the end of their adventures:

> So the harbor quickly filled up; it looked like the scene after the sea fight with Athens—these ships too were sailing back from battle decorated with garlands and with a Syracusan commander. The crews of the ships joined their voices to those of the people on shore in mutual greeting; the air was thick with blessings, cries of praise, and prayers, exchanged by both sides. Chaereas's father came too, fainting with the unexpected joy. Chaereas's friends from the young men's club and playing field jostled to welcome him. The women crowded around Callirhoe, who seemed to them to be lovelier than ever; you truly would have thought you were looking at Aphrodite herself as she arose from the sea. (8.6)

The tale ends with Chaereas in the theater recounting to the assembled citizens of Syracuse, men and women, how he and Callirhoe were separated and found each other again, while Callirhoe visits the temple of Aphrodite to thank the goddess for their safe homecoming.

Along with the emphasis on conjugal love in the romances comes an emphasis on the heroine.[19] Like the naive posturing of Kleitophon in the debate on pleasure, the heroine's steadfast defense of her virginity (or loyalty to her husband) is posed in terms that serve graphically to heighten the erotic charge of the narrative.[20] Consider the following scene in which another heroine, Leukippe, defends herself against the sexual advances of her owner when she is taken captive by pirates and sold as a slave.[21] She defies the man to use physical force:

> Bring on the instruments of torture: the wheel—here, take my arms and stretch them; the whips—here is my back, lash away; the hot irons—here is my body for burning; bring the axe as well—here is my neck, slice through! Watch a new contest: a single woman competes with all the engines of torture and wins every round ... Tell me, aren't you afraid of your goddess Artemis? You rape a virgin in the virgin's own city? Lady Goddess, where are your arrows?[22]

This scene bears an uncanny resemblance to one recurring in roughly contemporaneous martyr acts, where the Christian heroine declares her eagerness to face the torture threatened by a male executioner.[23] The posture of high-minded female abandon in the face of male aggression was clearly believed to capture a reader's attention.[24]

Even the exception to the rule of strict fidelity to the absent hero, Callirhoe's decision to accept a bigamous marriage to her new owner (she too is sold as a slave in the course of her adventures), is understood as a gesture of protection on behalf of the hero's unborn child, and is framed in terms of the reader's identification with her owner's desire (2.8ff). Indeed, Callirhoe is presented from the beginning of *Chareas and Callirhoe* as the possessor of a physical beauty so great that beholders think they are in the presence of Aphrodite herself, and the response of both men and women on first seeing her is one of voyeuristic awe.

The appealing heroine, described in erotically charged terms, provides a clue to the social location of the ancient romance. While in her vulnerability the girl serves as a narrative point of identification, her desirability serves as a point of objectification, a hook to capture the reader, all the more so if the reader is male. The fulfillment of desire between hero and heroine thus implicates the reader in the renewal of the social order which the romances propose.

To evoke desire in its quintessential element—the cravings of adolescence—was all the more effective where marriage was in view as a mechanism of narrative resolution. At a symbolic level, the craving for marriage served as a vehicle to propel a suspension and reassertion of established identity for both microcosm—the individual—and macrocosm—the city, or even the empire. At a literal level, what was also under discussion was marriage as a social institution. The peculiar power of romance to create complicity meant that an author could rely on readers to see in a tale of young lovers an allegory of the condition of the social order—and to be influenced by his views of how that order should be perpetuated. This power, and its usefulness to writers and readers alike, would outlive the ancient world itself.

"The More Storied the Better"

The texts themselves show a complex, self-conscious interest in the link between desire and representation. We see this strikingly in the frame story of the huntsman's visit to the shrine of Pan, noted above, which opens Longus' *Daphnis and Chloe*. The couple appear as young lovers in the main narrative, but in the frame story they are prosperous, married householders. We discover at the tale's end that the shrine so admired by our huntsman at the beginning—which occasions the tale itself—was commissioned by the couple as a gift to the place of their marriage. The reader who stops to reflect may be surprised by this conjunction of prosperous self-commendation and the rapture of young love: if we think of Daphnis and Chloe primarily as innocents within the world of the tale, our knowledge of that world is portrayed as the result of their patronage of the arts. We encounter them first at third hand, as civic actors, through an object they themselves have commissioned to mark their own nostalgia.

Although to us this unromantic view of romance seems to require explanation, Longus' contemporaries would not have been in the least surprised to see the most naive of young lovers put swiftly to work as socially useful householders and civic benefactors. What Longus' reader would have noticed, and delighted in, is the complex intersection of relationships between a tale and its human intermediaries, from subject to teller to audience. That Daphnis and Chloe might unproblematically figure both as goatherd and shepherdess and as legitimately married aristocrats went without saying; what was interesting was the problem of finding a local who knew the details.

This interest in representation, exemplified by the conceit of a narrator handing on a tale, and of the tale's unfolding from the description of a marvelous object, is a distinguishing feature of the literature of Longus' day.[25] *Leukippe and Kleitophon* opens with a frame story similar to that of *Daphnis and Chloe;* again, admiration of a work of art becomes the pretext for an extended narrative.

The narrator of *Leukippe and Kleitophon* is a visitor to the temple of Astarte, in the Phoenician city of Sidon, who encounters a stranger before a votive painting. The narrator strikes up a conversation by commenting on the figure of the god Eros in the painting, a representation of Europa and the bull. The stranger, Kleitophon, begins to expound on his own sufferings at the hands of Eros:

> At this point a young man standing nearby said, "How well I know it—for all the indignities Love has made me suffer."
>
> "And what have you suffered, my friend? You have the look, I know well, of one who has progressed far in his initiation into Love's mysteries."
>
> "You are poking up a wasps' nest of narrative. My life has been very storied."
>
> Well, sir, by Zeus and by Eros himself, please don't hesitate. The more storied the better." I clasped his right hand and we walked to a grove nearby where many plane-trees grew in dense array and a stream meandered, cold and clear as if from fresh-melted snow. When we had found a low bench to sit on, I said, "See, here we have the perfect spot for your story—a delightful place and a setting most appropriate for tales of love." (2)

Again we have a votive painting and a curious traveler delighted to meet up with "a wasps' nest of narrative," but this time the reader's curiosity is reflected in the narrator's expression of his own interest in the prospect of a good yarn. The expectation of love is deliberately confused with the pleasure of narrative, a fact that can hardly be disengaged from the author's own business of storytelling.

Writers from the second century on delighted in expanding on the self-conscious relation between a listener and the teller of a tale, or between a beholder and the object of his gaze. Thus Achilles Tatius reports a learned disquisition on the erotics of the gaze:

> You have no idea how marvelous a thing it is to look on one's beloved. This pleasure is greater than that of consummation, for the eyes receive each others' reflections, and they form therefrom small images as in mirrors. Such outpouring of beauty flowing down through them into the soul is a kind of copulation at a distance. (9)

Just as vision was endowed with particular sensuousness, so was narrative.

If objects and monuments were endowed with privileged readings, with histories to be discovered or hidden meanings to be unveiled, this meant that the man or woman in possession of the key by which to read forth these meanings was an object of curiosity and even awe. This was the era of philosophical allegory, which had arisen to mediate the clash of cultures resulting from the Hellenistic and Roman conquests. The phenomenon appears in all its seriousness in the explosion of allegorical readings in late antiquity of cultural icons from Homer to the Song of Songs.[26] But the interest in the encoded quality of visual and narrative representation was not limited to texts of a religious-philosophical orientation. It emerges across the spectrum of the literature of the later empire, in both Greek and Latin, from Pausanius' second-century handbook for the gentleman traveler to Apuleius' *Metamorphoses*, where a slave girl's mistaken understanding of the magical arts transforms a traveler into a pack animal, thus affording him a privileged standpoint of social invisibility from which to observe—and recount—the misadventures of those around him.[27] Curiosity about the world beyond one's city walls is indistinguishable from the sheer pleasure of narrative in these texts.

It is no coincidence that each of these narratives involves travel, for the displacement of an individual from his or her accustomed context also served to dispel any expectation that behavior could or should be calculated according to established patterns. In the context of a benign disruption of social expectations, the problem of interpreting signs and actions could be unyoked from the force of habit.

It would be useful to know whether the heightened sense of curiosity about the world "out there" in the literature of the later empire is a fantasy of escape from the oppressive weight of well-established patterns, or whether it is an attempt to make sense of a social context in which the patterns were vulnerable to erosion. It may reflect a dawning awareness of the limits of an identity constructed within the medium of a face-to-face society when the world beyond the walls of the city, with its unaccustomed opportunities and perils, is becoming increasingly accessible, even unavoidable.

Displacement and the curiosity it begets are the narrative end of romance's emphasis on travel. This may account for what is otherwise the anomaly of Longus' *Daphnis and Chloe*, the only ancient romance whose main action takes place entirely within an established community. Daphnis and Chloe both experience displacement through the discovery of unknown parenthood as well as through the power of love—like travel—to suspend the claims of habit.

Since love and disruption were linked in the ancient imagination, romance was a narrative form well suited to the exploration of the limits of an established identity. Generally it was expected that an individual's identity should be enacted within (and against) the confines imposed by his or her standing within a family and by the family's standing within the social order. The moment at which a marriage was contracted held enormous practical and imaginative significance, since it offered a fleeting opportunity for realigning a family's social and economic status. For parents, the period during which their child's marriage was arranged was fraught with anxiety, on the one hand, and heady with possibility on the other.[28] For the bride and groom, of course, the social consequences of marriage were all the more decisive, bound up as they were with a change in personal status within the family as well as with the alliance's effect on the larger dynastic system.

The ancient romance can thus be understood as a rhetorical echo chamber for the dynastic fears and hopes reverberating at the marriage feasts of the provincial gentry. In chronicles of the passage from tempestuous adolescence to the restabilizing foundation of a new household, ancient readers might enjoy the amplification—sometimes to comically grotesque proportions—of their deepest familial concerns. If at the marriage feast itself the guests had to endure a temporary suspension and readjustment of the social order, in consuming the fictional romance as readers the same group could indulge in an imaginative meditation on the moment of uncertainty. A complex literary incident of dislocation and renewal, the romance offered a fleeting view of a spectrum of alternatives to the well-considered behavior that neither reader nor author, it was tacitly assumed, would wish to disrupt in reality. But if the fictional romance was a safe vehicle for expressing—and gently mocking—the social trauma of renegotiating a family's boundaries and relationships through marriage, its status as fiction also served to remind readers of the fragility of their real-life pretensions. Marriage alliances were just as tenuous as the contracts of pleasure entered into between the authors and readers of romance.

What we see in the narratives is a restless and playful reflection on these themes, centering on the unpredictability of desire. It would be wrong to confuse this with a repudiation of the idea that duty and order should eventually be restored. The love that aspired to marriage involved a temporary disruption of the social order which led to its reassertion; other forms of love might pit the individual's interests against the common good. It was a well-known fact that men who succumbed to illegitimate desire might behave erratically, forgetting their responsibilities and noble intentions. Though such questions of desire, identity, and representation made for a good story, the emphasis in romance was on reconciling love to the common good.

Other late Roman writers were less interested in resolving the tension between desire and the social order than in the narrative threads that could be spun from desire's unpredictability. Thus, in the third-century *Dialogues of the Courtesans* by Lucian of Samosata, we find Pamphilus defending himself against his lover Myrtion's accusations that he plans to marry, by telling a tale of mistaken identity to account for how the false rumor was started (2).

Another of Lucian's dialogues, in which the courtesan Leaina explains to her colleague Klonarion the surprises involved in her new life as servant in the household of Megilla of Lesbos and her female lover, explores the disruption of identity through gender reversal. Leaina reveals to Klonarion the secret of Megilla's domestic identity: beneath a wig Megilla sports a shaved head, and at home the wig is removed and Megilla becomes Megillos (5). This kind of gender confusion crops up more than once in the *Dialogues of the Courtesans*. When the courtesan Pythias has her head shaved because of an illness, she is taken for a male rival by a client of her colleague Ioessa, who steals into Ioessa's room late at night after Pythias has removed her wig (12). The mechanism also recalls a scene in *Chaereas and Callirhoe* (1.4) where the hero disastrously mistakes the heroine's personal maid, whom he discovers in a midnight assignation, for Callirhoe herself.

In these tales we find a keen sensibility for the irony of a lovers' misunderstanding and for the interaction between illusion and reality that motivates desire. It is in the sphere of love that interruptions of identity find their most comic—and their most powerful—narrative expression. Where romance differs from other genres of the period is not in the exploration but in its proposed conclusion. We will return to the notion that romance could both indulge in such speculations and provide for their socially acceptable resolution.

Love among the Ruins

Still to be resolved is the relation of the romances to their historical moment. If not decadence, what accounts for their appearance? David Konstan holds that the Greek romance's "sexual symmetry," its stress on the reciprocal passion of its young hero and heroine, reflects the eclipse of the polis, "the city-state as a discrete social and political entity" (229). As the independent city-state gives way successively to the Hellenistic and Roman empires, Konstan argues, the literary representation of marriage signals the erosion of the old way of life. From the primary medium of dynastic allegiance and property transmission, marriage is recast as the end point of an individual quest by both male and female protagonists. Not insignificantly, the quest itself is largely understood as taking place beyond the walls of the city, constituting a travelogue of encounter with the myriad places and cultures of the empire itself.[29]

On this reading, the romance is a document of social devolution, an articulation of the changing place of the individual as the close-knit communities of the classical and Hellenistic period give way to the more impersonal social matrix of empire. This accounts for the persistent interest in questions of representation and identity. We watch, over and over again, as the romance's protagonists are thrust into unaccustomed situations that demand reassessment or concealment of the past. Similarly, the protagonists themselves are treated to first-person narratives by others who have encountered the unexpected in their travels. The characters meet as strangers, exchange stories, and move on to the next adventure. Konstan's suggestion is that the element of encounter here is the literary expression of increasing social alienation, an investigation of the "costs of empire," whether Hellenistic or Roman (an uncertainty necessitated by the uncertain dating of the genre).

The suggestion is valuable for its clue to the social imagination of the romances. Certainly the notion that an individual could be disengaged from his or her defining social position, and reviewed in a sequence of shifting contexts, would have held the interest of a population facing social change. But we should not feel obliged to dismiss the possibility that the impulse of the texts is deeply conservative. In a well-regulated traditional city-state, with marriages contracted between the family of the bride and her suitors to abet strategies for the transmission of property, an ideal of marriage based on romantic love would not necessarily be deemed subversive. Quite the contrary, it may have been perceived as an attempt to stabilize a founding institution of the social order by calling attention to its charms. Romance may result less from a freeing of social mores after the decline of the polis than from an attempt to stave off the decline by defending marriage. It is reasonable to think that such a defense occurred when the city-based conception of the social order, dependent on marriage both symbolically and concretely, was under siege—but we should remember that, in the minds of those responsible for its maintenance, the city was always under siege.

What this means is that we should not project an anachronistic puritanism into the minds of the fathers of the classical polis. The virtue appropriate to the married estate, *sōphrosynē*, implied well-measured enjoyment and not stark abstinence. The romantic celebration of desire in all its forms may be no less and no more than an attempt to remind the citizens of the Roman empire that while marriage and procreation were a public duty, the fulfillment of duty was not always unpleasant.

If travel represents the disengagement of the individual from the polis, then romance represents the ultimate reunion of the individual to common purpose, as the potentially antisocial force of desire is reconciled to the urgent civic necessity of biological and social renewal.

The obstacles to marital union faced by the protagonists, such as ship-wreck, capture by pirates, and temporary enslavement, signal the ten-uousness of the city's claim on the world around it. The chaste hero and heroine stand for the social order's regeneration, because it is un-derstood that their triumph over obstacles and their rejection of alter-nate sexual partners will find its natural end in marriage, and in the consequent householding and production of progeny.

What we have here is an enhanced version of a narrative that appears across the ancient world in contexts as diverse as founding myths, fertility cults, and epic.[30] Just as the philosophical (and pseudo-philosophical) texts we have seen were cast as a restaging of the debate of the *Symposium,* so the romances can each be read as a retelling of the *Odyssey,* where the restoration of the social order depends on the reestablishment of like-mindedness *(homophrosynē)* between Penelope and Odysseus after his return to Ithaca and the triumph over Penelope's suitors.[31]

With this in mind, we return to the frame story of *Daphnis and Chloe.* At the tale's close, the reader learns that it was Daphnis and Chloe themselves who "decorated the cave, and set up images in it and estab-lished an altar to Love the Shepherd, and gave Pan a temple to live in instead of the pine" (4.39). Longus' fictional huntsman draws an im-portant connection between his artless, nubile protagonists and the sober, prosperous men and women whose benefactions sustain the eco-nomic and cultural fabric of the ancient city.

In this way, the rustic shrine from which the tale stems is explicitly assigned a place among the tokens of memory by which the provincial gentry recommended themselves to posterity. It is this class of men and women, whose donations of marble and brick adorned each town center of the Roman Mediterranean, that we must bear in mind as we envision the now prosperous Daphnis and Chloe, reminiscing over their court-ship and dedicating a monument to the gods responsible for their hap-piness.

The metabolism by which the provincial town maintained its tradi-tional independence from the imperial center was always fragile. Its independence from Rome and its prosperity both depended on the flourishing of that class of men and women who were its principal benefactors. Much has been written in recent decades about the socioeconomic fate of the *curiales,* the regional aristocracy of the Roman empire, who, despite the general prosperity of the period, were already in the first stages of a long decline when Longus wrote.[32] Personally financed public benefactions, which notables such as the mature Daphnis and Chloe were expected to perform, had always been seen as both a privilege and a burden. Through the third and fourth centuries, the constant renewing of a town in the form of repairs to or new construction of municipal buildings, public baths, aqueducts, theaters, shrines, and fountains was increasingly perceived as a duty beyond the resources of the old provincial families, especially as new paths to prestige and power emerged through the centralized vehicles of imperial bureaucracy. Over time, the increments of urban renewal were handed over to the central government—often of course staffed by members of the same curial class—or to a Christian bishop, who himself increasingly came to represent an international hierarchy rather than an indigenous and autonomous body.

All this may account for the seeming wrong-headedness of viewing Daphnis and Chloe, the most famous young lovers of ancient romance, in light of their prosperous, possibly middle-aged afterlife as patrons of the arts: middle-brow literature offers a well-placed window onto the problems of provincial families. If the founding of cities and the maintenance of civic concord could be represented by the founding or re-establishment of a single household and the like-mindedness of its principal partners, then we can understand why these narratives held such interest, as cities began to give way to empire as the primary unit of the social order. The social order was by definition tenuous, and all the more so as one long-accepted articulation gave way to another, alien and still unstable. Although the ancient romance, interested as it was in the love problems of adolescents, might initially seem ill suited to a problem customarily approached from a political or economic angle, it may have been precisely the love problems of adolescents that symbolized the real anxieties—financial, not sexual—of the old families.

If this analysis is accurate, then the truism that the ancient romances reflect a situation in which "the world had become bigger, and the individual, in consequence, smaller in it—smaller, and more absorbed in himself, his private life,"[33] is almost precisely incorrect. Instead of self-absorption, forming allegiances is what the romance is about. It is also about encouraging the curial families, as they form those allegiances, to remember the interests of the city rather than dynastic ambition or self-preservation alone.

This added metaphorical layer is perhaps the most important one. As the young couple's reciprocal desire is turned to the purposes of the common good through marriage, so the interests of individual families give way to the needs of the city. We see this in its simplest version in *Chaereas and Callirhoe*, where the love of hero and heroine unites the interests of Syracuse's great political rivals. But directly beneath the surface is an implicit critique of the systemic competition among families through inheritance strategies such as infant exposure.

The situation in the romances is analogous to that described by Keith Hopkins for the aristocratic families of late republican Rome, where the dynastic interest of a single aristocratic family was best served by limiting reproduction—and thus the partition of its wealth among heirs—while the interest of the city was in a higher birth rate, both to replenish numbers and to prevent certain families from consolidating disproportionate wealth at the expense of their peers and the stability of the system. Hopkins cites the Stoic philosopher, Musonius Rufus, on this method of financial planning:

> What appears terrible to me is that some people, not even having the excuse of poverty, but being well-off *(euporoi chrēmatōn)* and some even rich, nevertheless presume not to nurture their children, so that the children born previously may be better off. They impiously contrive the prosperity of their children by the murder of their siblings; that is, they destroy their brothers and sisters, so that the earlier children may have a greater share of the inheritance.[34]

The stronger the ideology of marriage and fertility, the stronger the social pressure against such inheritance strategies as infant exposure, abortion, or discouraging other potential heirs from marrying while the primary heir survives.

Now consider the final scenes of *Daphnis and Chloe*. Here is the speech of the aristocratic Dionysophanes of Mytilene, having recovered the son he had abandoned as an infant:

> My sons, I married when I was quite young, and, after a short time, I had become, as I thought, a very lucky father. First a son was born

to me, and then a daughter, and thirdly, Astylus. I thought I had a big enough family, and when this child here was born to me, on top of all the others, I exposed him, putting these objects out with him not as tokens of his identity but as funeral ornaments. But Fate had other plans. For my oldest son and daughter died on a single day from the same illness, while you were rescued by divine providence so that we could have more hands to guide us in old age. Daphnis, don't hold it as a grudge against me that I exposed you; it was from no desire of mine that I formed this plan. And you, Astylus, don't be upset at receiving part of my property instead of the whole; to sensible men, nothing is more valuable than a brother. Both of you, love each other; as far as wealth goes, you can compete even with kings. (4.24)

The aftermath of this confession deserves further attention. Upon discovering that their newfound son Daphnis has pledged his heart to another foundling of marriageable age, the ravishing and therefore presumably aristocratic Chloe, Dionysophanes and his wife return to Mytilene in search of the girl's parents. There they hold a banquet for the Mytilean gentry—which is to say, all of the families with whom they would accept a marriage allegiance—and the tokens left with the infant Chloe are placed on a silver tray and carried round for the guests to examine.

Seated in the place of honor is the elderly Megacles. Recognizing the tokens, he explains his conduct in terms that evoke the plight of the curial class even more explicitly than the earlier speech of Dionysophanes:

At one time in the past, I had very little money to live on; for what I did have, I spent on public services, paying for dramatic choruses and warships. At that time, a little daughter was born to me. Shrinking from bringing this child up in poverty, I fitted her up with these tokens and exposed her, knowing that many people are eager to become parents even by this means. So the child was exposed in the cave of the Nymphs, paced in the trust of the goddesses; meanwhile, I became more affluent every day—now that I had no heir—for I haven't had the good luck to have any more children, even a daughter. (4.36)

Thus Chloe is reunited with her father and mother, and the next day the banqueters travel into the country to celebrate the wedding at the cave of the Nymphs, where Chloe had been left a foundling.

The account of the marriage feast is interrupted by a foreshadowing of the couple's future as icons of fertility:

> Not only then but for as long as they lived, Daphnis and Chloe spent most of their time living the pastoral life. They worshipped as their gods Nymphs, Pan, and Love, owned numerous flocks of sheep and goats, and thought that fruit and milk were the sweetest kind of food. When they had a baby boy, they put him under a she-goat for nursing, and when their second child was born to them, a little girl, they had her suck the teat of an ewe. They called the boy Philopoemen [friend of shepherds] and the girl Agele [herd]. They also decorated the cave and set up images in it and established an altar to Love *(Erōs)* the Shepherd, and gave Pan a temple to live in instead of the pine, calling him Pan the Soldier. (4.39)

The emphasis on rusticity should not be taken as a repudiation of the pair's new attachments in Mytilene, but rather as a symbolic reversal of the original abandonment. The needs of the city are equated with the rustic charm of its countryside: the son and daughter will share the primitive delights of their parents' childhood, and no other child is likely to suffer exposure for the sake of the family's economic advancement. Daphnis and Chloe are anchored to the values that best serve the city's interest precisely by their reluctance to abandon their rural estate, a variation on the theme of otium so pervasive in the literature of the Roman empire.

In bringing his narrative full circle, Longus also sets out an important clue to the social context of romance. Just as the innocent hero and heroine return to the scene of their marriage after the fact to dedicate gifts to the gods of the sacred grove, so in his prologue Longus himself offers his four books "to Love, the Nymphs, and Pan." That each work of art is an offering to the same gods is an important point in common between the books written by the lettered huntsman—by which Longus refers to his own narrative—and the benefactions of Daphnis and Chloe.

Thus Longus suggests, by comparing his own book to the gift of Daphnis and Chloe, that his act of writing should be understood within the context of curial benefaction (*leitourgia*). The analogy here between civic patronage and the writing of fiction is one to which we should pay close attention. We may infer that Longus' oblation to Eros is offered as part of his own obligation to the god and to the city. In this case, the refurbishment of a shrine and the writing of a romance are linked by their dedication to Eros, and their commemoration of the successful completion of yet another round of marriage negotiations for Mytilene's noble youth.

If such a tale was meant to offer light entertainment, it was also to serve a more serious social purpose. Romance has at its core the transformation of displaced persons into householders, of young lovers into legitimately married forbears of generations to come. With its warm appreciation of the strength of desire by which noble youths overcome the obstacles to legitimate union, the ancient romance was an opportune vehicle for making this point. That such a transformation took place by means of pleasure, whether for the hero and heroine or for the reader, should not be understood as compromising its serious intent. Pleasure, well-measured and harnessed to the common good, was understood by the ancients not to contradict but to ratify the actions of honorable men and women.

This may be what has been missing in the two decades since Veyne and Foucault reopened the question of conjugal love in the Roman period. The social dimension of pleasure in the ancient world was a matter of balance: though excessive indulgence in pleasure was perceived as a threat to the common good, so was its excessive repudiation.[35] A city needed, quite simply, a constant and plentiful supply of new citizens, and this could not be arranged in the total absence of pleasure. All the better if pleasure could be offered as a lure to the fulfillment of a vital task.

The romance's celebration of sexual passion, then, should be understood as an encouragement to fertility similar in aim to the Augustan marriage legislation that privileged fertile parents and pressured the divorced and widowed to remarry quickly.[36] Here the chaste desire of the legitimately married is privileged over other modes of sexual encounter, but the understanding is that the one cannot flourish without some benevolence toward the other. So the narrative of adolescent love serves both to symbolize the anxieties of families and cities as they negotiate the costs of empire and quite literally to remind the curial families that the empire depends on their fertility.

When we come to the literary descendants of the ancient romance, we will discover that it is precisely this aspect, the praise of fertility and of a social covenant symbolized through legitimately united sexual partners, which is emphasized. That it is twisted nearly beyond recognition may explain why so little attention has been paid to the Apocryphal Acts of the Apostles as a penumbral manifestation of the romance phenomenon. That the emphasis is shared, however, confirms the social function of the romance's insistence on individual desire. However inverted the terms, the Christian adaptations of romance represent an instinctive and powerful reading of just what was at stake in the genre.

When Christian writers of the second to fourth centuries came to challenge the probity of the ruling classes, the ideology of marriage as a union in desire of like-minded individuals would be the Achilles' heel to which they directed attack. It is to these writers, rather than to the patriarchs of the ancient city, that we must ascribe an ideal of denial, the antithesis of well-measured pleasure and the celebration of desire. The rhetorical economy of *sōphrosynē* and womanly influence, along with an ironic yet ultimately benevolent view of desire, continued in force among most Christians. But in the Christian literary language, romance serves to challenge the social order instead of reinforcing it. Desire remains, but its object is now a reunion with the divine and a return to the heavenly country, the homeland of the saints. The romance of late antiquity takes the form of a saint's life, in which the chaste desire of the legitimately married hero and heroine has metamorphosed into the otherworldly passion by which a Christian saint embraces a childless death.

· 3 ·

"The Bride That Is No Bride"

"I rightly see in you Eve repenting and in me Adam converting. For what she suffered through ignorance, you—whose soul I seek—must now redress through conversion ... You healed her deficiency by not experiencing the same passions, and I have perfected Adam's imperfection by fleeing to God for refuge. What Eve disobeyed, you obeyed; what Adam agreed to, I flee."[1]

Sometime around the turn of the third century, the Platonist philosophers Xenocharides and Leonidas are believed to have settled down to the work of recording the deeds of the apostle Andrew.[2] Among the many episodes of Andrew's travels around the Mediterranean, the most significant is his protracted encounter with Aegeates, proconsul of Acheaea, residing in the praetorium of Patras. It was Aegeates, our authors proposed, who was responsible for Andrew's death at Patras by lashing to a wooden cross. That it should have been a provincial governor who arranged for the execution is a realistic detail according well with the evidence from Pliny's letters for how the imperial bureaucracy handled persistent offenders against the codes of Roman *religio*—but the praetorium at Patras is a "historical" touch whose existence is otherwise undocumented. We can safely assume, then, that this version of Andrew's encounter with Aegeates has been altered (or perhaps invented) to accommodate a series of narrative exigencies. I will argue that the narrative strategy of the *Acts of Andrew* and the other Apocryphal Acts borrows from and inverts the ideology of *erōs* and the city's regeneration that we have seen in the ancient novel.

The Apocryphal Acts are insecurely dated, between the second and fourth centuries CE,[3] and relatively little is known of the circumstances of their production. But we know that the episodes about the preaching of continence were influential models for female piety in the centuries that followed. This means that an understanding of how the episodes functioned rhetorically might prepare the ground for a clearer understanding of the later texts that drew on them.

Two important triangles emerge in the *Acts of Andrew* as we know them. One, which would have been close to the hearts of Xenocharides and Leonidas if they were philosophers as well as Christians, was caused by the friendship between Aegeates' brother, Stratocles, "who had petitioned Caesar not to serve in the army but to pursue philosophy," and the philosophically sophisticated Andrew.[4] Stratocles rejects fraternal loyalty for the sake of the spiritual birth offered him by the apostle, and this substitution of allegiance highlights the contest between apostle and proconsul. In addition, Stratocles serves as a narrative foil to his more powerful brother. With Stratocles at his side, Aegeates is in a precarious position from the point of view of his ability to win over an audience. Unless he agrees with his philosophical counterpart, any attempt he makes to defend the Roman *religio* will be seen as a self-serving bid to defend his power against a morally superior challenger.

We see these elements at play even more strikingly in the triangle of Andrew, Aegeates, and Maximilla. When they are first introduced, Aegeates and his wife Maximilla might be taken as the hero and heroine of an ancient romance. After Andrew's arrival in Patras, his first healing miracle attracts the attention of the townsfolk.

> A few days later, Maximilla, the proconsul's wife, took sick. Despairing of the physicians who proved useless, she sent Iphidama [a trusted female slave] and summoned Andrew. "Holy Andrew," Iphidama said, "my mistress Maximilla, who is suffering from a high fever, asks you to come to her, for she eagerly desires to hear your teaching. Her husband the proconsul stands at the cot weeping and wielding a sword in his hand, so that when she expires he can stab himself with the blade."[5]

The explanation given for Maximilla's interest in the apostle is a fear that her beloved may be provoked to a rash act if she dies. The reasoning here is in the spirit of ancient romance, but the story takes a new turn almost immediately. After Andrew heals Maximilla, Aegeates offers a princely sum in payment. The apostle refuses, saying, "We received a gift, we give a gift. Rather, offer yourself to God, if you can." (*Liber de miraculis*, 30) The vehicle of opposition between Andrew and Aegeates is now in view, for it is Maximilla, not Aegeates, who will accept the apostle's exacting terms.

Aegeates is called away to Rome on imperial business, and Andrew befriends Maximilla and Stratocles (himself recently arrived from Rome). He proposes an alternative to the bonds of the family in the words of Jesus: "If you desire a father for those who are rejected on earth, I am your father. If you desire a legitimate brother to set you apart from bastard brothers, I am your brother" (*Passion of Andrew*, 12). When Aegeates returns, he finds that both wife and brother have reassigned their loyalty from the earthly to the heavenly household.

Now the narrative begins to play havoc with the conventions of ancient romance, preserving them, as it were, by inversion. Aegeates rushes into Maximilla's bedroom on his return and overhears her mention his name in prayer: he lavishes her with praise for wifely devotion and chastity. With the husband's expression of faith in his wife, the reader is invited to share in a joke at his expense. The real reason for her mentioning his name in prayer, we are told, is precisely the opposite of conjugal piety: "This is what Maximilla actually said, 'Rescue me at last from Aegeates' filthy intercourse and keep me pure and chaste, giving service only to you, my God' " (14). Thus begins a series of misunderstandings in which Aegeates is increasingly the object of Maximilla's cunning and scorn.

When Maximilla turns from prayer to greet her long-absent husband, her welcome is stern: "When he approached her mouth intending to kiss it, she pushed him back and said, 'Aegeates, after prayer a woman's mouth should never touch a man's' " (14). Taken aback, Aegeates retreats and Maximilla sends for the apostle "so that he may come here to pray and lay his hand on me while sleeping" (15). Andrew's prayer echoes Maximilla's own petition for continence, but his hostility to the husband is that of a rival in love:

> I ask you, my God, Lord Jesus Christ . . . may the spirit that is in her struggle even against Aegeates, that insolent and hostile snake . . . with respect to our savage and ever boorish enemy, cause her to sleep apart

from her visible husband and wed her to her inner husband, whom you above all recognize, and for whose sake the entire mystery of your plan of salvation has been accomplished. (16)

Maximilla's liberation from the conjugal debt, however, is portrayed as the result not of divine intervention but of her very earthly cunning. In a scenario worthy of the *Dialogues of the Courtesans,* she summons "a shapely, exceedingly wanton servant-girl named Euclia" and trains the girl so convincingly in impersonation that she is able for eight months to substitute for Maximilla in the marriage bed without arousing suspicion. Eventually Aegeates discovers the ruse and, grief-stricken, appeals to Maximilla, "I cling to your feet, I who have been your husband now for twelve years, who always revered you as a goddess and still do . . ." (22). By way of reply, she frankly acknowledges the erotic charge of her new allegiance:

> I am in love, Aegeates. I am in love, and the object of my love is not of this world and therefore is imperceptible to you. Night and day it kindles and enflames me with love for it. You cannot see it for it is difficult to see, and you cannot separate me from it, for that is impossible. Let me have intercourse and take my rest with it alone. (23)

Soon afterward, Aegeates has Andrew imprisoned.

When her husband makes one last attempt to win back her affections, Maximilla turns to Andrew for advice, and here we begin to understand the delicate balance in this narrative between sexual infidelity and the claim of sexual purity.

> "O Maximilla my child," Andrew replied, "I know that you too have been moved to resist any proposition of sexual intercourse and wish to be disassociated from a foul and filthy way of life . . . I bear you witness, Maximilla, do not commit this act. Do not submit to Aegeates' threat. Do not be moved by his speech. Do not fear his disgusting schemes. Do not be conquered by his artful flatteries. Do not consent to yield yourself to his artful wizardry. Endure each of his tortures by looking to us for a while, and you will see him entirely numb and wasting away from you and from all your kindred." (37)

And again:

Just as Adam died in Eve through his complicity with her, so also I now live in you through your observing the commandment of the Lord and through your transporting yourself to a state worthy of your essence. Scorn Aegeates' threats, Maximilla, for you know that we have a God who has compassion on us. (39[7])

What should attract our attention here is the way the contest between apostle and proconsul is couched in sexual terms.

A glance at the roughly contemporaneous *Acts of Peter* extends to comic proportions the metaphor of the contest between apostle and civic authority as romantic rivalry. Instead of one woman, Peter converts a series of different women, culminating in his encounter at Rome with the prefect Agrippa's four concubines, Agrippina, Nicaria, Euphemia, and Doris. In a touch reminiscent of Aristophanes' *Lysistrata*, the four women pledge to one another that none will satisfy the prefect's lust.[6] When the lovely Xanthippe, wife of "Albinus the friend of Caesar," joins their company, Albinus and Agrippa confer and decide that Peter must be executed.

Certainly provincial governors and other civic authorities made it their business to investigate the activities of Christians and sometimes condemned them to death. But there is no reason to believe that the fulfillment of this responsibility had anything to do with the governors' wives. It is not enough to assert, as most current scholarship has, that the erotic aspects of the narratives are there because the authors, wishing to promote asceticism, imputed sexual excesses to the enemies of a hero dedicated to renunciation. The emphasis on the apostle's continence may in fact reflect narrative strategy rather than the author's ascetic commitment. The apostle takes the place of the romantic hero, and since by doing so he must conquer the affections of another man's wife, it is no wonder that an attempt is made to establish his lack of interest in sex. If the heroine of the *Acts of Andrew*, Maximilla, has been married for twelve years, she is still only in her twenties, an age at which a stranger's repeated appearance in her bedroom would be considered suspect whatever his religious credentials. But why does the apostle set himself up as a competitor for her affections in the first place?

The answer, it is reasonable to suggest, lies in the link between the *Acts of Peter* and *Lysistrata*. It will be remembered that in Aristophanes' comedy, when Lysistrata and her cohort decide to organize a sex strike, their explicit goals are not sexual but political, to end a war that has become a matter of misplaced virility rather than of Greece's best interest. In the Apocryphal Acts, a similar narrative mechanism is occurring at the level of implicit meaning. That each woman hears the apostle's message and then desists from sexual relations with her husband can be understood as a form of protest against his handling of political matters, more specifically his unwillingness to recognize the apostle's preaching as a gift to the city rather than as a challenge to his own authority.

The inverted narrative similarities between the Apocryphal Acts and the ancient romances bear this point out. We see in the *Acts of Paul and Thecla* a more direct substitution of the apostle as romantic hero:

> And as Paul was speaking in this way in the midst of the gathering in the house of Onesiphoros, a certain virgin named Thecla, daughter to Theocleia and promised in marriage to the man Thamyris, seated at a nearby window of the house, listened night and day to the word of purity spoken by Paul.[7]

The image of Thecla, sitting by the window and straining to hear over the sounds of the street the voice of a man to whom she has yet to be introduced, reminds us of the scenes in *Chaereas and Callirhoe* or *Leukippe and Kleitophon* in which the hero and heroine encounter each other at a public gathering and are left pining, until they can be united in marriage.

Here, of course, what is at stake is not marriage but "the word of purity," in a context where purity clearly means sexual renunciation. Thamyris, the parentally approved fiancé of Thecla, is alerted to her change of heart and springs into action:

> Thamyris, hearing this and arising full of envy and anger, went away to Onesiphoros' house with the rulers and officials and a substantial crowd armed with clubs, and said to Paul, "You have corrupted the city of the Iconians and in addition my fiancée, so that she refuses me. Let's go to the provincial governor Castellius!" And the whole crowd said, "Carry off the magician! He has corrupted all our wives!"
> (15)

The wrath of Thamyris' *erōs* is not enough to restore his standing with Thecla, however. He brings Paul before the proconsul, who has him led off to prison. Thecla clings to the apostle with determination and manages to slip out of her house one night to visit him:

> But at night Thecla took off her armlets and offered them to the gatekeeper, and when the doors were opened for her she made off for the prison. And giving to the jailer a silver mirror she went in to Paul, and sitting at his feet heard the mighty works of God. And Paul was not alarmed, but exercised the right of a citizen to free speech on behalf of the Lord, and her faith increased as she tenderly kissed his fetters. (18)

The situation escalates to a full-scale public confrontation when she is found in Paul's cell, "bound with him in affection," by her family and Thamyris. The two are again brought before the governor, who questions her:

> And offering advice he said to Thecla, "Why do you not marry Thamyris according to the law of the Iconians?" But she stood looking intently at Paul. When she did not respond, her mother Theocleia called out, saying, "Burn the lawless one! Burn the bride that is no bride in the midst of the theater, so that all of the women who have been taught by this man may be afraid." (20)

Thus begins a cycle of martyrdom and miracle. Thecla is saved from death by divine intervention; she follows Paul into exile; they come to Antioch, and another man falls in love with Thecla and again has her brought before the governor when she refuses marriage. Again she is condemned, this time to the beasts, and again she is saved by divine intervention. She follows Paul to Myra, this time having converted the proconsul himself.

Each of these journeys—from Iconium to Antioch and again to Myra—is a long one: Thecla travels nearly the entire length of the south coast of Asia Minor twice, once unaccompanied, without parental consent. In one instance, Paul seems to disappear just when Thecla is most in need of assistance. The theme of her following after the elusive apostle is an echo of the long searches endured by the hero and heroine of ancient romance.

The Apostolic Love Triangle

That the Apocryphal Acts repeat a particular pattern of conversion to Christianity, one in which a triangle forms between a woman, her marriage partner, and the apostle whose preaching she wishes to follow, has long been acknowledged. What has not been established is what kind of relation obtains in the narratives between the call to continence and the call to social or ideological change. The rivalry between two men over the allegiance of a woman formed the central narrative outline, but it is not immediately apparent whether the apostle's proposal of sexual abstinence was understood by an ancient reader as an end or only as a means.

If the parallelism between the Apocryphal Acts and the ancient romances is intentional—and surely it must be—then the rejection of the romance's ideal of passionate marriage was also a response to the romance's call for renewal of the city. The substitution of apostle for marriage partner in the heroine's affections means that the persuasive force of desire is being put to a new purpose. We will see too that the position of the heroine as listener to the apostle's word adds a new twist to the rhetoric of womanly influence: now the woman is not speaker but audience.

It should be remembered that the generic expectations of the ancient romance signaled the heroine's fiancé or husband—not the apostle—as the rightful hero. Similarly, the traditional view of marriage as "a rampart for the city," expounded by the unsympathetic husbands, fiancés, and marriage-conscious mothers in the Apocryphal Acts, would have been the prevailing view among Christians right up to the end of antiquity. This would have been increasingly true as the Christian movement continued its drift toward respectability. Ascetic practice was by definition the predilection of a minority, but ascetic heroes and heroines exerted an influence disproportionate to numbers. The ascetic ideal was widely tolerated, even celebrated, by many who had no intention of heeding its claims. In this sense, ascetic language stood poised between revolution and irrelevance.

The rivalry between the two pretenders to the heroine's allegiance follows a more or less standard pattern in the tales. In the *Acts of Paul and Thecla,* the encounter between fiancé and apostle is immediately negative; in other instances the relationship is initially positive because of the apostle's ability as a healer. In both the *Acts of Andrew* and the *Acts of John,* the apostle encounters a Roman magistrate[8] on the brink of suicide because his wife is incurably ill. In the *Acts of Andrew* it is the wife who sends for the apostle, and the healing leads to her conversion and a rift with her husband.[9] The *Acts of John* seems to have two versions of the paradigm, one in which it is the husband who begs the apostle to "glorify your God by healing her"; both husband and wife follow the holy man.[10] A second version, whose beginning has not been preserved, may or may not include the elements of healing and of the husband's status, but it registers discord between the husband Andronicus and the wife Drusiana over the apostle's preaching. That the Drusiana episode begins with her conversion and her husband's resistance is evident from a fragment in which Andronicus figures as an unbeliever, found in a Manichaean psalm book.[11] In addition, an episode in the preserved *Acts of John* refers to Drusiana's conversion to continence when yet another man falls in love with her:

> people said to him, "It is impossible for you to get this woman, for she has long ago separated even from her husband for the sake of piety. Are you the only one who does not know that Andronicus, who formerly was not the god-fearing man he is now, shut her into a sepulchre, saying, 'either I must have you as the wife I had before, or you must die!' And she chose to die rather than commit that abominable act." (63)

The *Acts of Thomas* and the *Acts of Paul and Thecla* preserve the element of the husband's high social status and civic responsibility, although the stories depart from the pattern of the wife's healing. The ninth act in the *Acts of Thomas* records the encounter of the apostle with "Mygdonia, the wife of Charisius, the close kinsman of the king," and the eleventh with Tertia, the wife of King Misdaeus himself. Both meetings result in unilateral continence on the part of the wife and in opposition between the husband and the apostle.[12]

The *Acts of Paul* preserves yet another variation, differing in the fact that Thecla is not yet married and in the duplication of the encounter. Her repudiation of Thamyris brings her and Paul before the proconsul at Iconium, but her miraculous deliverance leads to a restaging of the conflict, when another man in Antioch causes her to be condemned to the arena because she rejects his advances. In both cases, the element of continuity with the other Apocryphal Acts lies in the power and civic rank of the men who desire her.[13]

By this duplication, the *Acts of Paul* makes clear the usefulness of the heroine's continence as a narrative device to propel the conflict between the apostle and a symbolic representative of the ruling class of the cities he visits. The husbands, fiancés, and suitors of the women who embrace continence are almost all described as men who have it in their power to threaten the holy man (or his new convert) with martyrdom, which casts the apostles in the best possible light, their opponents in the worst.

The unsuccessful attempts to persuade the heroine to accept the conjugal bed and her place in the social order may offer a clue to the meaning of these episodes. The speech of Aegeates to Maximilla in the *Acts of Andrew* plays on the importance of marriage to social continuity by emphasizing its intergenerational aspect: "Maximilla, because your parents thought me worthy to be your mate, they pledged you to me in marriage without regard to wealth, heredity, or reputation, considering only the kindness of my soul" (36[4]). Again, in the *Acts of Paul and Thecla,* we witness the dismay of Thecla's mother, Theocleia, when the daughter is transported by the preaching of Paul of Tarsus and refuses an advantageous marriage to Thamyris. The mother is mocked for siding with the jilted fiancé. Here is Theocleia consulting with Thamyris:

> For three days and three nights Thecla has not risen from the window either to eat or to drink, but gazing steadily as if on some joyful spectacle she so devotes herself to a strange man who teaches deceptive and subtle words, that I wonder how a maiden of such modesty can be so sorely troubled. Thamyris, this man is upsetting the city of the Iconians, and your Thecla in addition . . . like a spider at the window bound by his words, she is dominated by a new desire and a fearful passion. (8–9)

There is little sympathy in this text for a mother's sense of betrayal or for her assessment of the preaching of continence as a challenge to the ancient city as she knows it. Rather, it is precisely because of Theocleia's thoughtless complicity in the demands of the city—its craven, seemingly endless need to harness the bodies of its youth to replenish its numbers—that she emerges as one of the story's minor villains.

A few lines later, Thamyris and Theocleia are devastated when they recognize the gravity of what Thecla intends. The heroine herself is supremely unresponsive:

Those who were in the house wept bitterly, Thamyris for the loss of a wife, Theocleia for the loss of a daughter, the maidservants for that of a mistress. So there was a great confusion of mourning in the house. And while all this was going on Thecla did not turn away [from the window], but gave her whole attention to Paul's word. (10)

In an ordinary romance, the episode of the heroine spellbound by a traveling *magos* would not seem out of place, but that the girl should never recover would be some cause for alarm. The expectation is clearly that the audience will identify with the heroine's rejection of her duty to family, city, and empire. But we know from the tombstones of countless chaste wives throughout the Roman empire that such duties to past and future generations were valued as much by Christians as by pagans.[14]

An important chapter in the history of the city in late antiquity, and of the encroachment of Christianity into its life, is bound up in the rhetorical antithesis—highlighted by competition over the allegiance of a pure woman—between the well-meaning but spiritually inadequate householder and the visionary Christian ascetic. In the Apocryphal Acts we find both continuity and subversion: continuity, in that the heroine established in the ancient romance appears again in relatively unchanged form; subversion, in that the traditional hero's position is insecure, and he eventually loses the heroine to a man who is clearly his superior but whose goals are not those of the social order. Thus we move from a celebration of sexuality in the service of social continuity to a denigration of sexuality in the service of a challenge to the establishment. This is why in the Apocryphal Acts wives (or fiancées) must refuse the marriage bed and why husbands (or fiancés) must be politically powerful.

The challenge by the apostle to the householder is the urgent message of these narratives, and it is essentially a conflict *between men*. The challenge posed here by Christianity is not really about women, or even about sexual continence, but about authority and the social order. In this way, tales of continence uses the narrative momentum of romance, and the enticement of the romantic heroine, to mask a contest for authority, encoded in the contest between two pretenders to the heroine's allegiance.

The narratives have been referred to as "chastity stories,"[15] a misnaming that reveals the rhetorical sleight of hand at work in the stories. For these texts precisely do *not* celebrate *sōphrosynē*—chastity—the virtue proper to a devoted, and fertile, wife, celebrated by the ancients as the female counterpart to male self-mastery. Instead they celebrate heroines who substitute for *sōphrosynē* the potentially antithetical virtue of *enkrateia*, continence. The fifth-century *Life of Syncletica*, for example, would argue that the married are not capable of *sōphrosynē* at all but only of its opposite, *aphrosynē*, folly.[16] The rhetorical question such texts pose might be phrased: if chastity (avoidance of fornication) is good, is not continence (avoidance of sex altogether) better? The classical answer to this question—and the answer of most Christians— would have been decidedly negative. But for the purposes of apologetics, the rhetorical question was effective.

The Hero's Austerity

The task, then, is to understand how and why the Apocryphal Acts dwell so forcefully on the theme of sexual renunciation. The traditional answer has been that the Acts were a fringe phenomenon, emerging from the ranks of the uneducated.[17] One scholar has put forward the theory that the *Acts of Paul and Thecla* is part of an oral tradition, possibly handed down by women, certainly by the dispossessed.[18] But our ancient evidence refers to the Apocryphal Acts as recorded by men of learning, whether Platonist philosophers in the case of the *Acts of Andrew* or the literate priest whom Tertullian adduces as the author of the *Acts of Paul and Thecla*.[19] That they were understood in this way by other ancient writers, combined with their close connection to the Greek romances, suggests that the emphasis on sexual renunciation—in contrast to the romance's stress on fertility—was the product of literary and rhetorical sophistication. On this reading, the inversion of romance is intentional, not coincidental.

By contrast, much early Christian literature shares with romance the ideal of temperate marriage as an index of a male leader's social responsibility. Within the New Testament canon, both views are represented. This is how the author of the Deutero-Pauline epistles, writing during the late first or second century, puts it: "a bishop must be above reproach, the husband of one wife, temperate, sensible, dignified, hospitable," or again, "let deacons be the husband of one wife, and let them manage their children and their households well" (1 Timothy 3.2, 3.12). The more or less contemporaneous Book of Acts and the genuine letters of Paul, written a generation or more earlier, record the importance of married couples in the early Christian missions.[20] But the heroic type of the charismatic preacher is the ascetic man who calls others to renounce their place in the social order, as he himself has done (Matthew 19.21, for example).

This difference has been accounted for by the hypothesis that an early, radical vision of the Church, in which asceticism and charismatic authority reinforced one another, gave way over time to an institutionalized version of Christianity, which no longer had to challenge the social order because it had itself *become* the social order.[21] Ascetic renunciation was symbolic: "the human body is never seen as a body without being treated as an image of society."[22] The mind-body duality, in this interpretation, serves as the medium through which the relation of the individual to the wider society is represented. Where the body is denigrated, this means a rejection of the demands of society in favor of the autonomy of the individual.

But a complimentary reading, that of rhetorical analysis, produces a surprisingly different result. To a reader familiar with the classic literature produced by the ascetic communities of the fourth and fifth centuries, the ascetic claims of the second- and third-century Apocryphal Acts—and even of the canonical New Testament—are striking in their emptiness. The preaching of continence appears in these texts, but as a cipher. We see none of the interest in the substance of asceticism that pervades the sayings of the desert fathers or the writings of John Cassian. What we have in the Apocryphal Acts is an interest not in asceticism per se but in the threat to established authority posed by an outsider who is patently superior in moral and ethical terms.

Thus the recourse to a description of the hero's ascetic views in these texts would then have been first and foremost as a rhetorical weapon. Whether or not the earliest Christians abhorred embodiment, it was in their interest to represent their leaders as scorning the pleasures of the body, if only because attachment to these pleasures was the undisputed source of strife among individuals and among communities. Embodiment and its trappings, usually represented by sex or money, were the area in which individuals, families, and communities could expect harm—or at least competition—from one another. Even power itself was figured in terms of embodiment, as a claim on behalf of the epitome of carnality, one's progeny.

To advertise one's own (or one's hero's) immunity to the addictions of embodiment was to claim not only a palpable moral superiority, but even an immunity to the accusations of moral excess which were regularly levied among claimants to power. A man who had neither heirs nor desire to produce them could be represented as one on whom the demands of self-interest laid no claim. Ancient readers would have understood these claims as a powerful manipulation of the rhetoric of *sōphrosynē*, which may explain why the Roman aristocracy found ascetic practices "objectionable and threatening."[23] Austerity, in the sense of self-control, was a good thing, but it was good because it was temperate. The pressure exerted on men to conform to a shared culture of *sōphrosynē*; represented the reintegration of a single man, and of a single household, into the body social as merely one more among equals. But taken to an extreme, self-control was no longer a sign of equality and community: even self-denial could signal an antisocial self-assertion.

Rhetorical analysis adds a new dimension to the theory of ascetic behavior as "performances designed to create a new culture and to inaugurate a new identity."[24] The rhetorical approach to asceticism pushes back the terms of the definition to another discursive level: *accounts* of ascetic behavior themselves become performances, designed to elicit a new sense of allegiance from an audience. The chronicling and advertisement of ascetic behavior at all levels, from abstinence to defiance in the face of death, served as a medium for claims to power and allegiance. The invention of the ascetic hero and heroine was an important element in the formation of a Christian alternative language of power and society.[25]

So the parable of the wandering ascetic and the settled householder would have been recognizable to an ancient audience as an exploration not of asceticism but of Christianity's claim to moral superiority, with the figure of the ascetic teacher representing a disinterested challenge to the status quo. Whereas the language of *sōphrosynē* was meant to maintain the social order, the language of asceticism was meant to disrupt it.

Both the proponents and the critics of an ascetic model of authority knew this, portraying those in power as standing for the status quo and the otherworldly outsider as standing against it. (That is, all parties cast the debate in terms of relative position and vested interest.) Critics suggested that the otherworldly themselves aspired to power, that they were arguing for the downfall of the current system in order to install their own faction—or, even worse, to abet their private interests. Lucian of Samosata's third-century satire *The Death of Peregrinus* offers a disturbing perspective on the willingness of Christians to place their resources at the disposal of an outsider whose self-proclaimed virtues might not be genuine and who might not have their best interests at heart.

The assertive function of the outsider is of course an old story. In its most simplified form, it leads us to read the Christian apologist's claim to moral superiority in much the same way as the sociolinguist reads the behavior of the twentieth-century teenaged hero:

> The rebellious youth who turns into an authoritarian adult is a commonly observed paradox . . . "Born rebels" who defy authority are not oblivious of it, but oversensitive to it. Defying authority is a way of asserting themselves and refusing to accept the subordinate position. When they are old enough, or established enough, to take the dominant position, reinforcing authority becomes the way to assert themselves, since the hierarchy is now operating to their advantage.[26]

Thus the claim to otherworldliness implies a view of self and society which is original only for the technique of its claim to power—that the rhetoric of otherworldliness is not only this-worldly in its aims, but dangerous for its hypocrisy and its capacity for annexing the moral high ground to dubious ends. (We are not far in spirit here from the Roman critique of Plato discussed earlier.)

This position has of course been argued memorably by Marx and Nietzsche, who were themselves building on an argument of Rousseau:

> Now as this new idea of a kingdom of another world could never have entered the minds of pagans, they always regarded the Christians as

true rebels who, under the cloak of hypocritical submission, only awaited the moment to make themselves independent and supreme, and cunningly to usurp that authority which they made a show of respecting . . . What the pagans feared did indeed happen; then everything altered its countenance; the humble Christians changed their tune and soon the so-called kingdom of the other world was seen to become, under a visible ruler, the most violent despotism of this world.[27]

It is important to distinguish our own project from Rousseau's. Although—or perhaps because—it is immediately gratifying, dismissive cynicism does little to explain how otherworldliness actually functions as a claim to power, and it may even foreclose sustained analysis by its participation in the cycle of claims and accusations.

Seen in rhetorical terms, the connection between ascetic behavior and social protest operates at many levels. First of all, it is an enhanced version of self-mastery as a coin of competition for status. As an apologetic strategy, it made sense for Christians to claim that their movement was characterized by this kind of moral prowess. Symbolically, ascetics were men who could be trusted to exhibit self-control when faced with the temptations that might lead a lesser man to betray duty or to appropriate what belonged to another: paradoxically, an exhibition of supreme self-control (and a corresponding absence of covetousness or excessive craving for power) was precisely the token by which Christian accession to power could be bought.

At the end of the twentieth century, it is perhaps less easy to imagine the attraction and potential explosiveness of claims to moral superiority. Such claims have always been deployed by the proponents of new religious or political affiliations. To gauge the vast scale at which these claims can operate, it may be useful to recall their decisive importance in the outcome of the Chinese civil war (1946–1950). Performances of moral integrity and reminders of Kuomintang corruption were critical to the Communists' ability to win over the local communities whose support was vital to an eventual victory.[28] The Communist tradition of austere personal conduct still has its critics in East Asian capitalist governments, in whose eyes the rhetorical magnetism of the Communist language of personal austerity even now constitutes a political threat.[29] So, too, we know from the early apologists and from the martyr literature that the conjunction of self-abnegation and tenacity was revered by Christians. It is tempting to imagine that these qualities were revered—as in modern China—at least in part for their capacity to discredit an opponent and to annex, along with the moral high ground, the widespread support of a people long accustomed to corruption and hardship.[30]

What the Apocryphal Acts explored, then, was how the established relations of power could be undermined. If the romances were about maintaining the stasis of the ancient city, the Apocryphal Acts were their antithesis, narratives designed to highlight the clash between the man of authority and his morally superior challenger. The established man's passion for the heroine, instead of representing a renewal of the city, came to represent the social order's claims on those who found them intolerable.

To clarify the link with apologetics even more, a useful comparison can be made with Justin Martyr's *Second Apology,* written in the middle of the second century, a generation or more before the Apocryphal Acts. Justin opens his apology, addressed to the Roman Senate, with the case of three condemned Christians: Ptolemy, Lucius, and an unnamed woman. The woman had been married to a drunken and debauched husband, "given to all kinds of unnatural and unjust pleasures" (2.4). Initially she shared his life of vice, but on receiving instruction from the Christian Ptolemy, she renounced worldly pleasures and enjoined her husband to do the same, persuading him with salutary threats of "the hell-fire reserved for those who live without *sōphrosynē* and contrary to the true logos" (2.2). Despite many attempts to reform him and fearing that she herself would be party to his crimes if she remained in the household, the wife finally served him with divorce proceedings.

> The good and great man ought to have rejoiced that his wife, who had once lived a licentious life among servants and hirelings, given to drunkenness and all manner of evils, should renounce it and wish that he do the same, but, not wanting the divorce, he brought the charge against her, that she was a Christian. (2.7)

Justin goes on to explain how, having initiated proceedings against the wife, the husband then turned his rage against her teacher and was able to have Ptolemy condemned to prison on the same charge of being a Christian. Now the third man, "a certain Lucius," enters the picture.

Present in the crowd at Ptolemy's hearing, Lucius expresses his outrage that such a paragon of morality should be condemned because of his faith. His expostulation only serves to identify Lucius himself as a Christian, and thus all three are condemned.

In this anecdote, we can see clearly that the Christian woman's dissolute husband is adduced precisely to illustrate the bad faith of the man who opposes the Christian message, and to demonstrate that his motive is not at all, as the Senate might imagine, a concern for civic order, but in fact the sordid motive of preserving (and abusing) his own dominant position. The figure of the Christian wife serves to emphasize, in an explicitly apologetic context, Christian vulnerability and moral excellence by comparison to the complacency and vested interest of the powers that be.

Sexual Renunciation and the Romantic Heroine

If this reading is correct, it would contribute to the erosion of a hypothesis, popular a decade ago, that the Apocryphal Acts were intended by their original authors as "expressions of a woman's world."[31] We should remember that Stevan Davies, who brought forward this line of argument in 1980, drew explicitly on Erwin Rohde's now discredited assumption that the Greek novel was intended for a female audience, arguing by analogy that the Apocryphal Acts were at the very least produced for a female readership if not by female authors.[32] More recent studies have begun to explore the variety of purposes to which the emphasis on women within these texts might have been put by male authors.[33]

Again, as in the case of the ancient romance, a more sophisticated approach is beginning to emerge to the possible configurations of relationship between an imagined world and its real-life authors or audiences. For the second and third centuries, we possess only glancing evidence for the readership of these texts (although we will see that evidence for who read them and why abounds from the late fourth century on). We have no way of knowing even whether the texts reflect a paradigm of wives-first conversion that was understood to exist in social reality, or whether an ancient reader would instantly recognize it as an obviously literary (and possibly comic) stereotype. Scholars as dissimilar in date and approach as Arthur Darby Nock in the 1930s and Ross Shephard Kraemer a half century later would have agreed that, when ancient accounts indicate that women were the first to embrace the new faith, this should be taken as a matter of verisimilitude.[34] But now it is possible to speculate that ancient writers dwelled on the trials of a virtuous heroine for literary, rhetorical, and even quasi-pornographic reasons.

An important clue to the role of the heroine in these narratives is her polar opposite in early Christian gender stereotyping: the garrulous old woman. Dennis MacDonald argued a decade ago that the warning pre-served in the Pastoral Epistles to "avoid the profane tales told by old women" (1 Timothy 4.7) was the key to the authorship of the more or less contemporaneous (and geographically proximate) *Acts of Paul and Thecla*.[35] Important for our purposes is not MacDonald's hypothesis, that the Thecla narrative was recorded from an oral tradition preserved by female storytellers, but the link between Thecla and the type, pre-served in many ancient sources, of old wives who spread falsehoods.

Irenaeus of Lyons, for example, whose *Against Heresies* is roughly contemporaneous with the *Acts of Paul and Thecla* (and perhaps with the Pastoral Epistles, if the very late date proposed by MacDonald is accepted), makes a similar charge against suspect groups.[36] Old women were particularly easy targets for this rhetoric, because of their role in the households of the Roman empire as ubiquitous, low-status child-carers.[37] The philosopher Celsus, seeking a vivid image to characterize the Christians as tellers of falsehoods, made it clear that old women were the paradigmatic purveyors of nonsense: "Would not an old woman who sings a story to lull a child asleep have been ashamed to whisper tales such as these?"[38]

We are in the presence here of a highly charged rhetorical polarity. The continent heroine is essentially not a speaker but a listener. Her reluctance to speak serves both to amplify the truth of the apostle's word and to mark her as a point of identification for the audience. If false-hoods were associated with the uncontrolled speech of old women, the rapt listening of feminine youth and purity were linked to the truth. The attractive, aristocratic, attentive young virgin was the type of the ideal listener, straining after truth, and the repulsive, lowly, garrulous, and jaded old woman was the type of the suspicious speaker. For the apostle to preach continence to a willing female listener served as an overarching metaphor for the Christian mission, whether or not the preaching was actually taken as a substantive call to continence.

If we imagine the continent heroine as an idealized listener, we can come one step closer to understanding how the new, heroic continence changed the terms of the classical rhetoric of *sōphrosynē* and womanly influence. At one level, Maximilla as "Eve repenting" in the *Acts of Andrew* is equal and opposite to the empress Eudoxia as "Eve persuading" in the *Lives* of John Chrysostom, within the same narrative economy. Both are married to powerful men against whom the Christian hero must defend himself; both cases draw on the image of Eve, the archetype of womanly influence. We are not far here from the polarity between Cleopatra and Octavia as exerting womanly influence— negative or positive—on the public man.

But in the case of Maximilla, Eve does not turn her influence to the good. The wife does not persuade her husband but instead abandons him. Insofar as actual historical advice by Christian clerics to married women is recorded, it suggests the reverse, that wives married to insufficiently Christianized husbands were expressly forbidden to neglect the opportunity their influence gave them to serve the Church.[39] But for the purposes of Christian fiction, persuasive speech was the prerogative of the hero. The attentiveness of his female listener amplified his message and reflected glory on his heroism.

The one sliver of contemporary evidence we possess for the authorial intent behind the Apocryphal Acts suggests that this was so. A passage from Tertullian of Carthage suggests that, in the case of the *Acts of Paul and Thecla,* enhancement of the hero was the author's intent; when the text fell into the hands of female readers, however, some of them proposed a different reading of the heroine. Be it a lack of cultural sophistication or a deliberate, self-interested blind eye, something led at least some women to see the Christian heroine not as an icon of obedience to the apostolic word but as a precedent for women's clerical authority.

In *On Baptism* Tertullian warns against a group of women who not only serve as Christian teachers but also claim the right to baptize:

> But if they claim writings which are wrongly inscribed with Paul's name—I mean the example of Thecla—in support of women's freedom to teach and baptize, let them know that a presbyter in Asia,

who put together that book, heaping up a narrative as it were from his own materials under Paul's name, when after conviction he confessed that he had done it from love of Paul, resigned his position.[40]

The passage goes on to remind the reader that the Paul of the New Testament canon had in fact argued *against* female teachers (1 Corinthians 14.34–35), despite the insistence in the *Acts of Paul and Thecla* that he had personally enjoined Thecla to "Go and teach the word of God" (41).

To suggest that certain female readers discovered in the *Acts of Paul and Thecla* a meaning incongruous with what was intended by the author may seem incautious, since the evidence for authorial intention is already so slim. But that is just what Tertullian says: the male presbyter who wrote the book meant to exalt the apostle, but some female readers saw it as license for female authority within the Church. What we know about how readers construe meaning from texts supports the idea that they may find a message very different from what the author intended.[41]

We see in the female readers whom Tertullian deplores a new, perhaps specifically Christian, style of reading, in which readers search the story for a figure who shares their own identifying characteristics and judge their own status accordingly. From the late fourth century on, abundant evidence testifies to this practice of reading for identification and ranking. For women, the heroines of the Apocryphal Acts, Thecla in particular, would serve an especially important role as icons of self-understanding.[42]

Renunciation and Audience

Thus the romantic heroine is an ambiguous figure as she appears in the Apocryphal Acts. On the one hand, her substitution of ascetic for romantic partner suggests a substitution of otherworldly for worldly authority, of apostle for proconsul. A subversion of genre expectations, including the sleight of hand between chastity and continence, made it possible for a single male figure to possess the charisma of the outsider—the purveyor of otherworldly values—while standing in for the romantic hero, the insider in training, in whom civic hopes were traditionally placed. This may have been what the learned presbyter of late second-century Asia Minor who compiled the *Acts of Paul and Thecla* "for love of the apostle" had in mind.

On the other hand, the same moral purity could be used to subvert the established authority of the Church itself, just as the Church used it to challenge the pagan status quo. This would have been so for the second-century women who claimed Thecla as a precedent for a female clergy, and it would account for why the Apocryphal Acts were intermittently condemned as heretical, even as orthodox bishops paid fulsome tribute to their heroines.

This may explain the early Christian emphasis both on ascetic heroes and on the seemingly contradictory model that takes the married householder as the paradigm of ethical fitness. To stress a connection to men and women of ascetic power was to look outward to the boundary between Christianity and other religious communities, to assert Christianity's claim to moral superiority; to stress more traditionalist notions of moderation was to maintain order within the group itself.

This brings us back to the problem of how texts that lionized continence and the repudiation of marriage could gain an audience beyond those who actually intended to subvert marriage and the household. The answer lies partly in the civic ranking of the protagonists. In the ancient novel, the hero and heroine are the darlings of the provincial aristocracy; in the Apocryphal Acts the distraught parents and jilted lovers are viewed without sympathy and even with satisfaction. In the *Acts of Andrew*, it is the household of the imperial governor—the emblem of centralized Roman exploitation of the provinces—that is in question; in the *Acts of John* Lycomedes is "praetor of the Ephesians," presumably a magistrate prorogued to the provinces at the end of his term of office; and of course Peter's antagonists in the *Acts of Peter* are the praetor in office and a friend of the emperor himself. While not all of the husbands or fiancés in the Apocryphal Acts are linked in this way to the imperial administration, the outline that emerges shows a ruling class that has not captured any hearts.

Perhaps a useful way to characterize the difference between the ancient romances and the Apocryphal Acts is in the treatment of the curial class. The Greek novel, written if we can believe Longus by and for provincial families, sought to distribute their wealth more evenly and so to reinforce the social order by luring readers toward the duty of procreation. But the Apocryphal Acts paint an unsympathetic picture of the men who governed the ancient city. A shift in identification has taken place: from an exploration of the difficulty of maintaining an evenly distributed cadre of reasonably wealthy and literate landowners, to an assertion of resentment against the politically powerful. The shift is not necessarily in the readership. As the representative of a central political power, a proconsul such as Aegeates would have been resented even more by his provincial colleagues than by the less privileged. The Apocryphal Acts reflect and even encourage the envy and resentment for the disproportionately powerful that the ancient romances had been designed to obviate by fostering an even distribution of wealth.

For the period of their production, the second and third centuries, we may never be able to document the audience of the Apocryphal Acts and the other novelistic figments of the early Christian imagination, beyond noting that they seem to expect an audience familiar with the belles-lettres of the age but resentful of the imperial administration. Still it is clear that in the late fourth century, when the romances of renunciation finally reached the daughters of consuls and governors, their appeal was irresistible. Imitation of the heroine became the vehicle of identification for female audiences, and the gesture of sexual renunciation took on an increasingly well-documented importance as a model for women of all classes.

It would be injudicious to suggest that aristocratic women had not been exposed to the Apocryphal Acts earlier, since there is no evidence one way or the other, but there is evidence that, from the mid fourth century on, women of the curial class and indeed of the senatorial aristocracy encountered these writings in unprecedented numbers. This apocryphal vogue helps to explain how a patently antisocial vision of religious heroism at the expense of civic duty could capture the allegiance of precisely that class of citizens for whom civic duty had a defining importance, the senatorial class of Rome.

· 4 ·

An Angel in the House

"When you were carried fainting out of the funeral procession, the crowd was whispering thus: 'Isn't this what we often said? She weeps for a daughter killed by fasting, because she will not have grandchildren from her [the daughter's] second marriage. How long before these detestable monks are driven out of Rome, are stoned, are thrown into the Tiber? They have seduced a wretched *matrona;* that she is not a nun by choice is proven by the fact that even among the pagans none has ever wept so over her children.' "[1]

These are the words of an eminent biblical scholar, writing to console an aristocratic widow over the death of her twenty-year-old daughter from what might now be understood as the aggravated symptoms of anorexia. The letter stands as a prelude to the disgrace and departure from Rome of one of the most brilliant men the Latin Church had known. In the autumn of 384, Jerome, the writer of the letter, was a man at the peak of his powers. He had recently returned to Rome after a long absence and garnered unparalleled accolades for his zeal and learning at the papal court and among the aristocratic laity. Some months before he had begun a stunningly ambitious project, the revision and retranslation of almost all of the existing Latin Bible, a project whose result is the core of the Vulgate version as we know it. The death of Blesilla, the daughter of Paula, his social and literary patroness and his most intimate friend, must have seemed to be nothing less than a major family tragedy and, at the same time, nothing more. In hindsight, however, it was a turning point, for roughly a month later, on 11 December 384, Damasus, bishop of Rome, met his death as well.

Damasus, the author of the learned poems on the early Christian martyrs still inscribed in stone or set in mosaic in many a Roman catacomb and basilica, was Jerome's literary mentor and his guarantor. His death left Jerome unprotected from the ill will of those who envied his abilities or despised the brazen self-assertion by which he had found favor at the papal court. The death of Blesilla was widely understood as resulting from the immoderate program of self-mortification that Jerome had urged on the girl during a period of fragile health; the responsibility for her death was laid at his door. To those who felt that no good could come from Jerome's pose as the arbiter of ascetic rigor among senatorial ladies (whose acquaintance ought by rights to have been judged beyond his station) there could be no surprise in the tragic outcome.

Less than a year later, Jerome fled Rome for Palestine. By then, allegations about the death of Blesilla were the least of his worries. The shadow of opprobrium had fallen on his relationship with Paula, the bereaved mother. That his intimacy with the widow had become the occasion of scandal is confirmed by a letter to his friend—and Paula's— the ascetic Asella, written from the seaport at Ostia on the eve of his departure in August 385.[2] A formal charge of seduction seems to have been brought against him and, although subsequently dismissed, it rendered bleak his prospects of any future place in the Roman church.

While they no doubt served as a distraction to outraged matrons in the torpor of a Roman August, the details of Jerome's disgrace need not concern us here. What we must examine are the terms in which Jerome chides the grieving Paula, for they are a measure of the distance between Jerome and the generations before him. They are words whose fourth-century resonance we must strain to catch if we want to understand the change in cultural equilibrium wrought by the conversion to Christianity of the senatorial class.

Jerome's report of his critics casts his friend and patroness Paula in an unsympathetic role. The satire derives much of its rhetorical power from the Christian tradition of ridiculing the wish of parents to marry off their children young and well, a comparison that, even if directed to his critics, would have compromised Paula too. Jerome certainly knew the tradition; indeed, elsewhere he assures Paula's other daughter, Eustochium, that if she follows his instructions on how to fulfill the virginal ideal, on the day of reckoning Thecla of Iconium, heroine of the *Acts of Paul and Thecla*, will fly into her embrace.[3]

To call on the image of Thecla to justify a daughter's asceticism was an established commonplace by the end of the fourth century. Thus Gregory of Nyssa's biography of his eldest sibling, the *Life of Macrina*, reports the visionary experience of their mother Emmelia during childbirth:

> And when the time came for her to unleash the labor pangs in childbirth, she fell asleep, and seemed to carry in her arms the child still embraced in her womb, and someone appeared in image and figure befitting a great man, and called the little one in her arms "Thecla"— that Thecla, who is renowned among virgins. And after doing this and witnessing three times, the vision disappeared, and gave her an easy labor, so that when she awoke from her sleep, she saw that the dream was real. And so this was the child's secret name. But it seems to me that the vision did not say this to guide the mother in naming the child, but rather to foretell the life of the girl and to call attention to the similarity between her choice of life and that of her namesake.[4]

The parent who perceived the value of a child's ascetic vocation, then, was granted visionary confirmation. The parent who failed to do so was dismissed as spiritually inept.

An anonymous Greek *Homily on Virginity* addressed to parents phrases the problem thus:

> Often when a daughter yearns to strive for higher things, the mother, concerned for her children or misled by their imagined temporal beauty, or perhaps consumed by jealousy, tries to make her daughter a child of this age and not the one espoused to God. All wicked things imaginable set traps; but do not flinch in fear, my child! Lift your eyes upward to where your Beloved is; follow in the footsteps of that famous one who has gone before you and of whom you have heard: Thecla . . . even if Theocleia is troubled and Thamyris laments, even if Alexander overtakes you, even if the judge threatens you, let nothing extinguish your love.[5]

Although the sermon is explicitly addressed to the parents of prospective ascetics, at this point the writer calls on the young girl herself, suggesting that her unenthusiastic mother be cast in the role of Theocleia, mother of Thecla.

Similarly, we see in the *Life of Melania the Younger*, written between 440 and 453,[6] a chronicle of the heroine's repeated efforts to shrive herself of the responsibility of marrying and producing an heir for her family's vast estates. Although her family is Christian, the terms in which her resistance to the familial claim on her fertility is drawn are those of the Apocryphal Acts.[7] Though we know little about the authors or readers of Christian romances of the second and third centuries, by the late fourth century we can begin at least tentatively to trace both. Texts such as the *Life of Macrina*, the *Life of Melania*, and the letters of Jerome have identifiable authors and readers, and even relatively certain dates of composition. Once the literature of asceticism attains an identifiable aristocratic readership, it is possible to register the tensions elicited by the figure of the aristocratic-ascetic heroine.

Thus—not coincidentally—it is precisely as they are undergoing a shift in social location that we first begin to find substantial external evidence for the composition and readership of ascetic narratives. We cannot be sure that second- and third-century men and women projected the same questions and problems into these texts. But it is instructive to watch the process by which fourth-century readers and writers negotiated their meaning.

Let us remember for a moment the passage in the *Acts of Paul and Thecla* to which the anonymous *Homily on Virginity* refers, and which most closely corresponds to the situation evoked in Jerome's letter to Paula. There too we saw little sympathy for a mother's loss of her daughter, and Jerome's mockery of those who held him responsible for Blesilla's death can be understood only with reference to the pattern of hostility to familial claims set out in Christian romance. The suggestion that at Blesilla's funeral his critics indulged in narrow-minded carping over the loss of yet another potential mother of the city's heirs served to paint those critics in an intentionally unflattering light.

By implying a comparison between Blesilla and Thecla, and especially in a letter exhorting the dead girl's mother not to grieve, Jerome steers perilously close to a comparison between his own beloved Paula, the mother of an ascetic daughter but herself an ascetic of no mean repute, and Theocleia, the mother of Thecla, known to history only for her inability to recognize the importance of Saint Paul's preaching. Such an insinuation, however impalpably it was fostered, was calculated to strike at Paula's heart.

Rhetorically, the insinuation served to remind Paula that her social standing and material prosperity might be cast in a similarly unflattering light if she were to balk at Jerome's advice regarding the position and wealth that so vexed her spiritual progress and that of her remaining offspring. This clearly did him no harm in his relations with Paula, who cheerfully followed him into exile and financed his ascetic ambitions for as long as she lived. But Jerome's appeal to a Christian tradition of ridiculing the hopes that aristocratic families placed in their progeny, even as he was addressing a noblewoman who was herself Christian on the subject of her own dead child, betrays his penchant for the slippery edge. It was a calculated risk: by airing his disdain for those worldly advantages that others possessed and he lacked, he might level the ground between himself and his social superiors, whether opponents or allies. Should the strategy fail, on the other hand, he left himself open to being dismissed as a canting arriviste.

The stakes were high for Jerome, and for those around him. His brief sojourn in Rome took place at a time when the Christian population was in the midst of a radical demographic shift. In leaving Rome, Jerome was leaving behind a Christian audience that had come to include the social peers of those proconsuls whose anxieties an earlier Christian literature had the leisure to ridicule. The Faith had begun to count among its most ardent practitioners the daughters of Rome's illustrious families. With the arrival of the ascetic vogue among the aristocracy, the Christian tales of an aristocratic heroine and her struggle to extricate herself from the bonds of marriage and family came to have a new social meaning. The rhetoric of asceticism—and its appeal to the figure of the continent heroine—had been designed for addressing an audience that precisely did not include the elite group at the center of imperial power.

When we consider the reception of the ascetic romance in these circumstances, it is the changed dynamics between fictional dramatis personae and actual readership that we must chart. G. D. Gordini reminds us that Jerome's praise of Marcella—who had taken him on as a protegé early in his Roman stay—as the first Roman noblewoman to embrace the monastic way of life, does not suggest that Marcella was the first female ascetic in Rome, but rather the first of her class.[8] The terms of the praise may in fact be stereotypical, since Eustochium figures in Jerome's Letter 22 as the first noble virgin,[9] despite the existence in her own circle of Asella, whose veiling as a virgin probably took place before Eustochium's birth. (In Eustochium's case, the adjective *prima* could also be a term of preference rather than of chronology.) In any event, Gordini suggests that the order of virgins was well established in the west by this time, but that the mid-to-late fourth century saw an increasing participation by aristocratic women.[10] It was asceticism's new prominence among the aristocracy, not the appearance of asceticism itself, that constituted a change in Rome.

To understand Jerome's denigration of marriage and procreation is beyond the scope of this study. Yet his invective raises a series of important issues about the social place of the ascetic movement at Rome and the social tensions its success among the powerful would have elicited.

We still have to account for women's participation in the ascetic movement. Why their participation would have been desirable from the point of view of the men whose virtue their presence reflected is evident—but why the women's own interest in the venture? In the next chapter we will look at the views of those cautious souls who did not participate in the new vogue of female asceticism. Here our task is to understand the enthusiasts.

A substantial literature has arisen over the past two decades directed to understanding what women found attractive in a symbolic system that emphasized their humility and innocence. The most useful answer to date has been framed in terms of power: by renouncing an open claim to worldly power, women were able in exchange to gain personal autonomy and even enhanced social authority.[11] This model, which has gained wide acceptance, is almost certainly correct in its main emphasis.

We will find, however, that more can be said once this interpretation is in place. There is a danger of drifting toward one of two poles, romanticism or reductionism, either one of which precludes further discussion. The reductionist view—a more or less Nietzschean position—would be to view the use of renunciation to gain power as cynical or manipulative. Conversely, the romantic view would assume that power was unavailable to women when asceticism was introduced. This view depends on a "strawman" conception of women's disempowerment in the pagan or traditionalist Christian contexts, so that their position in the ascetic movement might seem the lesser of evils (an approach that has been challenged when applied to ancient Judaism[12]). Both views are unsatisfactory. What remains is to devise a language for discussing the rise of asceticism that takes account of power relations without viewing them strictly in romantic or reductionist terms.

A Language of Christian Identity

This segment of our story began with the 380s because of the issue of documentation. But to understand the context for the arrival of asceticism among the well-documented ladies and gentlemen of the imperial capital, we must look back to the beginning of the fourth century, to what is often referred to as the Constantinian revolution. We will see that a daughter's renunciation of the world carried a meaning in many ways similar to the Victorian ideal of domestic womanhood,[13] with the added dimension that the girl's vow of virginity signaled the family's noble scorn for the matter of earthly riches and an open-hearted embrace of the angelic life of the world to come.

Almost immediately after the emperor Constantine's rise to power, beginning with the Edict of Toleration of 313, we see changes in the imperial legislation on religious affiliation. As early as 320, there is a suspension of the provisions against celibacy of the Augustan marriage laws.[14] This was surely the result of the high esteem in which the desert ascetic movement of Egypt was already held by such well-informed and influential men as Eusebius, bishop of Caesarea from 313 to 339, and Athanasius, bishop of Alexandria from 328 to 373, whose biography of the desert father Antony spurred the ascetic conversion of the young Augustine and countless others.

We should also recall an important factor of a very different kind. From 313 to 320, a sweeping change in the legal status of bishops took place. On one hand, bishops and clergy were progressively granted immunity from the economic responsibilities that weighed on the curial class; and on the other, bishops were granted a civic status equal to that of magistrates, including the right to adjudicate legal disputes.[15] Of a sudden, to accept ordination to the clergy or consecration to the episcopacy was no longer to risk one's life. Over a period of less than ten years, it became a low-cost vehicle for upward mobility through a curial class burdened by debt. The effect of these changes was not felt immediately, but over the course of the century city councils relinquished much of their power to the episcopal courts.[16] Since clergymen were expected on the whole to marry and beget offspring, the deft ordination or consecration of sons would fit well into the financial planning of a family on the rise. This was not the intent behind the legislation: Constantine seems to have understood the early fourth-century clergy as a group whose low social status and lack of earning power made them economically vulnerable.[17] But given the increasing prestige and real power of the episcopal office, there was an understandable influx of the ambitious into the Church.

From this influx arose the subtlest and most pervasive of the dangers faced by the fourth-century Church. How did one distinguish between the servants of God and the servants of Mammon? It is a problem that troubled the Church from the very beginning. We know from a first-century church manual, the *Didache*, that a dishonest profit could be turned by the unscrupulous from even the most unstructured version of charismatic leadership; the problem was far more serious when abuse of the credulity of the faithful was a matter not of a night's lodging but of exalted civic office.

This is not to say that the fourth-century episcopacy was a population of charlatans. Even honest, well-intentioned men of the cloth might have been pleased to benefit from a situation they saw as incidental to their higher purpose. But it was cause for concern. We can imagine that when a man such as Ambrose, governor of Aemilia-Liguria, was elected bishop of the imperial city of Milan in November 373, his enthusiasm for the ascetic life was read as a reassuring message that he did not mean to exploit his position for dynastic ends.[18]

We know too, from Ammianus Marcellinus, that among the laity certain great families were believed to have outstripped their peers in wealth by unscrupulous maneuvering for the favor of Constantine and his heirs.[19] When in her early teens Anicia Demetrias, heiress of the same family on whose misappropriation of wealth Ammianus had cast aspersions,[20] announced her decision to take the veil, the congratulations that poured in from around the Mediterranean must have been motivated in part by relief.

A daughter's innocence held a place of considerable importance in the late Roman imagination. Strikingly, it is in the same discussion of rapaciousness and court intrigue in which he censors the greed of Demetrias' forbears that Ammianus includes this characterization of Constantius II's fear of assassination:

> Constantius, rather faint-hearted and anxious for his life, and always expecting a knife at his throat, was like Dionysius, the famous Sicilian tyrant, who was led by the same failing to have his daughters trained as barbers, because he would not trust anyone else to shave him. (16.8.10)

An unmarried daughter was the only person who could be trusted to hold a blade to a ruler's neck without being tempted to clear a place for a rival's ambition. This vivid image encapsulates a number of significant elements in late Roman thought. A family's relations with other families and a man's relations with other men were often characterized by a disavowal of intent to take advantage of another's trust and by a watchful eye against the other's betrayal. Sons were the fundamental unit of danger: a son's future was the likely repository of a man's dishonest intent, and yet the son's impatience for power or wealth might endanger the father himself.

The unmarried daughter, by contrast, served to symbolize family loyalty uncompromised by any motive for betrayal. Her power, at times a force to be reckoned with, existed only insofar as it harnessed the perceived moral authority of this bond of loyalty. It lent to the daughter's virginity a sacred aura. Married, a daughter stood for a family's compromise with the dynastic needs of other families, its concession to them of heirs. Unmarried, the virgin stood as a symbol of all that was uncompromised and unmixed in affiliation, and thus by extension of all that was true.

Of course it was not the Christians who invented the sacred symbolism of the virgin. The cult of the hearth, tended in each house by a daughter's purity, was as old as the *Iliad*, and the fire of Hestia, the virginal hearth goddess, was still tended by the thirty virgins of Vesta in Rome.[21] At one level, the Christian adoption of this mode of sanctity was an attempt to furnish the *plebs dei* with some of the rich complexity of religious identity available within the polytheist system. Certainly the deacon-presbyter-bishop trinity represented a diminution of agency for women, but for both sexes it represented a winnowing of what had been an endless variety of roles, identities, and agencies in standing before the gods.[22] Countless specific religious titles are preserved from the ancient world which scholars have yet to identify.[23] But whatever the nature of these roles, the fact remains that there was scope in the polytheist system for a wide variety of individuals to participate in one cult or another as "specialists." The spare, hierarchical elegance of the episcopal system, which aroused the envy of the emperor Julian, may have been vital to an embattled religious minority, but once the heroic danger of the persecutions had passed, Christians were left with a paucity of roles for shoring up their sense of religious identity.[24]

Even if the oppositional status of the Church within the Roman empire obfuscated this flaw in the Christian polity, we can already see during the persecutions a consciousness of unease among the rank and file. During the pestilence of 252 at Carthage, the bishop Cyprian faced a congregation dispirited not by the threat of death itself—Carthage had produced more than its share of martyrs—but by the prospect of a danger to which no hallowing interpretation was assigned. These were men and women who felt that to suffer the torments of martyrdom was an honorable and even a glorious destiny, but their composure failed at the prospect of a suffering unmitigated by any well-structured identity. Cyprian's response to the situation, the treatise *On Mortality,* is a masterful attempt to reinterpret the Christian Church as a federation of spiritual warriors whose individual battles with the demons of self-doubt and discouragement are as important to the polity as the visible achievements of its acknowledged heroes. But where later writers would draw repeatedly on Cyprian's vision, the Church remained parsimonious in providing opportunities for self-expression and identification to its broad membership. There was a danger that such a polity would attract only the spiritually austere and the affectedly sanctimonious, without drawing in the good-natured middling sort.

In this close atmosphere, the ascetic movement created a refreshing opportunity for novelty and role play. This is not to dismiss the honest intentions of its adherents, but merely to suggest that it made available a new source of narrative and identity with which the laity could experiment until they found a type and degree of intensity to suit them. For women, this would have been all the more welcome given their limited access to participation in the clerical hierarchy.[25]

When Ambrose of Milan defends his right to prevent the families of consecrated virgins from forcing the girls into marriage, it is in terms of the Church's rich diversity. The vow to virginity may not be revoked for the greater claims of marriage:

> A field bears forth many fruits, but the better field overflows with both fruit and flowers. Such a field is the Church, fecund with varied bounty. Here you may discern the seeds of virginity in full bloom; there widowhood, standing powerful in its seriousness, as if in an orchard; elsewhere, the Church's marriages, like a cornfield filling the world with its fertile harvest, or like a wine-press of the Lord Jesus overflowing with the produce of the marital vineyard, where the faithful fruit of marriage abounds.[26]

He also argues that virginity has a particularly important role to play because of its affinity to the heavenly life:

> I ask, then, whether this [virginity] is censured as improper, as new, or as unproductive. If as improper, then the vows of all are improper, improper is the life of the angels, for "those who neither marry nor take wives will be like the angels in heaven" (Mt. 22.30). Hence, whoever censures this, condemns the Resurrection. (6.27)

It was Ambrose who catapulted the virginal ideal to prominence in the Latin Church, and it was he more than any other who found in virginity a key for interpreting the biblical literary heritage as a rich mine of possible identities for the faithful.[27]

Jerome's Letter 107, written in 403 to Paula's daughter-in-law Laeta, shows how a daughter's innocence could unite a family across the lines of religious affiliation:

> Who would have believed that the granddaughter of Albinus the pontiff would be born in answer to a mother's vows, so that, with the grandfather present and rejoicing, the still stammering tongue of the baby might sound "Alleluia," and even the old man nurse in his arms a virgin of Christ? We did well to wait for such a day. A holy and faithful household sanctifies the one unbeliever.[28]

The letter goes on to describe in loving detail every aspect of how Laeta's daughter should be brought up. The picture is one of a life resonant with scriptural allusion:

> After she has begun to be a bit larger, and to grow in wisdom after the example of her Bridegroom, and in age and in the favor of God and other people, let her make her way with her parents to the temple of her true Father, but let her not depart the temple with them. Let them seek her upon the path of the world, amid the crowds and the company of kinfolk, and let them find her nowhere but in the inner sanctum of the scriptures, informing herself about her spiritual marriage through the prophets and apostles. (7)

One can imagine the sense of enhanced identity that both the child and her family would have experienced in their dealings with the Church. To consecrate a daughter's virginity afforded a family a privileged point of contact with church structure and tradition while affirming time-honored ideals of filial piety and innocence.

When it was a matter of a girl's own choice, the same factors were at play. A number of letters are preserved that congratulate aristocratic virgins of marriageable age on their decision to take the veil. These stress the importance of meditation on the Scriptures and the discovery there of confirming echoes of one's own experience. Jerome's Letter 22 to the virgin Eustochium—Paula's daughter and Laeta's sister-in-law—begins by invoking Cyprian's image of the life of faith as an eschatological battle. Jerome continues by turning to his own ascetic struggles in his years (374–376) as a hermit in the Syrian desert. The effect of introducing this first-hand experience would be to invite the girl's imaginative participation in the heroism of the desert movement, which excited great curiosity at Rome and Milan in those years. (Jerome is writing four years before Augustine's second-hand encounter with the *Life of Antony*, recorded in the *Confessions*.)

He invites her to withdraw into a private world constructed from the imagery of the Song of Songs:

> Let the hidden places of your bedroom always keep you, and let your Bridegroom always be at play with you inside. You pray: you are speaking to your Bridegroom; you read: He is speaking to you, and, when sleep overtakes you, He will come behind the wall and put his hand through the opening, and he will touch your belly, and, trem-

bling, you will arise and say, "I am wounded by love" (Song of Songs
5.8). And in reply you will hear from him, "My sister, my bride, is an
enclosed garden; an enclosed garden, a sealed fountain."
(*Letter 22.7*)

Whatever our own reaction to such advice, delivered by a man in his
forties or fifties to a girl, we cannot dispute that it would have offered
Eustochium a sense of privilege and identification in her encounters
with the sacred text.

We see in Pelagius' letter to Anicia Demetrias, the granddaughter of
Petronius Probus, on her taking the veil (c. 414) a careful analysis of
the problem of encouragement:

> Whenever it falls to me to speak about principles of character for-
> mation and the cultivation of a holy life, I usually point first to the
> vigorous properties of human nature, and make a case for what it is
> capable of achieving. In this way, I incite the mind of the listener
> toward an idea of virtue, so that no one thinks he is asked to pursue
> an impossible goal. By no means can we enter the path of the virtues
> unless we are led by hope as our escort. This is because commitment
> to strive toward a goal suffocates in the despair of attaining it. It seems
> to me that this plan, which I have held to in other writings, is all the
> more to be observed here. The greater the goodness one affirms in
> nature, the more perfect the life one may teach: for otherwise, the less
> the mind believes itself to be capable of, the more sluggish it may
> become and the more negligent in the pursuit of virtue, and what it
> unknowingly possesses, it believes itself to lack.[29]

The letter to Demetrias is generally read as a manifesto of Pelagius' views
on free will, and such a reading is not inaccurate. But it is at the same
time an attempt to grapple with a problem that troubled the Church
over the course of the fourth century. A means had to be found for
distinguishing between Christians of serious purpose and Christians in
name only. It was important to discourage the latter and even more
important to avoid demoralizing the former by a lack of encouragement.

Asceticism and Social Prestige

"Look at how the daughters of noblemen behave, look at how they carry
themselves; look at their careful education . . . inspired by their sense

of high birth, they rise above the ordinary behavior of mankind . . . by habitual discipline, they have created in themselves a nature different from the common run of men."[30] Christian writers of the late fourth and early fifth centuries would discover that this means of assuaging the tensions within the Christian polity brought its own problems: it was impossible to avoid a certain amount of jockeying for status among the seekers after perfection. The problem was exacerbated by the changing contours of the body of the faithful. The authority of religious heroes had always stood in tension with civic authority—the acts of the martyrs are the prime example. Yet with the influx of the senatorial aristocracy into the Church in the fourth century, the otherworldly hierarchy of religious heroism and the worldly hierarchy of civic position and patronage had to be reconciled.

One of the curious aftereffects of the transformation of the senatorial aristocracy from the Church's enemies to its allies was that, for the first time, the claims of Christian religious authority to outrank civic authority found an audience among some of those who actually held civic power. Essentially, the competition was transformed from a fictional competition (important perhaps in the collective consciousness of Christian communities) to a collision in earnest between authority systems.

Asceticism's new place among the aristocracy would have attracted criticism first because of the jarring contradiction of unworldly ambition and worldly success. In addition, it was in Rome that asceticism faced an especially conservative, even a skeptical response:

> one imagines that it was particularly Rome which reserved for the new way of life a cold and hostile reception. The three major Catholic opponents of monasticism found a venue for their theories precisely here, which suggests that the movement's progress was not easy. The same conservative and traditionalist spirit on the part of the Roman Church, even when refraining from disapproval, tended to regard the new with caution.[31]

The Roman critics of asceticism found a wide audience of sympathetic listeners among the socially responsible and the politically powerful.

Now we should return our attention briefly to the whispering critics at Blesilla's funeral, the women and men of the Christian community who were unsympathetic to the idea that young women of the senatorial class should be encouraged to put into practice the fiction of the aristocratic virgin sworn to continence. To begin with, it seems safe to say that these critics were themselves part of the ruling class. Whereas scholars have acknowledged on the basis of Jerome's report that the congregation at Blesilla's funeral included critics of the ascetic movement, they have in a sense mistaken Jerome's cue, by thinking of the whisperers as disreputable rabble and not as women and men upholding responsibility for the well-being of a community and its individual members.

Jerome's method of raising objections only to dismiss them can help us to reorient our perception of his opponents. If his characterization of the critics at Blesilla's funeral can be understood as a recourse to the early Christian commonplace of ridiculing first families, as suggested above, it is reasonable to imagine that these critics were located within that sector of the laity whose concern to perpetuate the social order was both its hereditary right and its duty: the senatorial aristocracy. They seem to have understood themselves not as non-Christians but as Christian traditionalists, a point that modern scholars have been slow to apprehend. To these aristocrats, the ascetic way of life seemed marked by an unwillingness to consider the common good.

It would have been to Jerome's advantage to invoke the specter of Theoclia and her kind if this were the case. Not only would it serve as a mild threat to Paula of the precariousness of her position, but it would serve to accuse his aristocratic critics of insufficient conversion to Christianity, by implying that in their social conservatism they were hard to distinguish from their pagan counterparts.

From a rhetorical point of view, it was a brilliant move, for in the 380s the conservatives still held sway.[32] They saw the social dangers of too enthusiastic a reception for the ascetic ideal, correctly perceiving in asceticism a competing system of social ranking that, if it did not eradicate the aristocracy's traditional claim to position, would permanently alter its terms. The concern to preserve a religiously positive role for married couples, and a socially positive role for married women, would indeed have been shared by Christians and pagans alike. If married women felt bound to acknowledge the prestige of virgins, this would undermine the old civic associations that had centered on concord between husbands and wives. Marital concord (real or invented) had been the sign that a family's economic and political power was well deserved and would be used for the public good. It was a conception of power that relied on long-held notions of aristocratic self-control. Those who defended it were heirs to a claim (and indeed to a sense of duty) that their actions should reveal them as better than their social inferiors—now their coreligionists, comprising the Church's at-large baptized membership—not only in standing but in their very nature.

To perceive the social danger these men and women saw in the ascetic movement, we should return to the question of social mobility. It was not only that a new criterion for social ranking would allow men and women to form allegiances outside their established place in society. Far more threatening was the idea that, as the canons of the old order were being challenged, no commensurate mechanism for regulating social relations was emerging to take their place. This is a point to which we will return. First we should consider social mobility from the point of view of the ascetics themselves.

Female Ambition

In a 1987 study, Anne Ewing Hickey challenged the prevailing hypothesis that what attracted women to the ascetic life was the prospect of social advancement. Hickey argued that, in the letters of Jerome, her major source, the ideology of female monasticism was a direct heir to the ideology of self-effacement and self-sacrifice characterizing the classic Roman wife. What she offered in place of advancement as an answer to the question "What was in it for women?" was a sociological interpretation. Following Talcott Parsons' theory of social action, Hickey suggested that the attractiveness of asceticism to aristocratic women could be explained in terms less directly connected to social status: rather than promotion to a new level of freedom or power, asceticism offered a sense of structure and definition in a period of social uncertainty.

What I propose is a realignment of the social-advancement hypothesis that also takes into account the importance of social structure and self-definition. To begin with, we should remember that if the language used for women's claims to ascetic advancement was a language of self-effacement, this does not necessarily mean that ascetic success conferred no social prestige. In fact, as we will see, ascetic accomplishment was expressed precisely in terms that evoked an existing ideal of woman-hood, one traditionally aligned with power and prestige.

In addition, it may be a mistake to attempt to distinguish conclusively between prestige or social advancement, on one hand, and a sense of definition and identity on the other. In the face-to-face society of late imperial Rome, identity *was* prestige. So when we look for social advancement among ascetics, it is misleading to look for the kinds of freedom or autonomy that might emerge in a postindustrial society. The medium of prestige in our texts was a certification of moral authority, a *bonum* whose potency—and susceptibility to abuse—in the late Roman social context should not be underestimated.

We see already in Jerome's letters that ascetic achievement had become a way for senatorial women to assert their social standing—in part, one imagines, because it reduced their household expenses and made lavish donations possible.[33] Correspondingly, ascetic practice became a way for non-aristocratic women to claim a kind of religious authority that was enhanced by its senatorial associations. Further, since not all senatorial women could claim the dignity of ascetic virtue, deftly publicized ascetic achievements may have allowed some individuals to trump their social betters. This raised a query: were women converting to asceticism for the sake of virtue or for the sake of being *seen* as virtuous?

That ascetic writers themselves were concerned to distinguish between ascetic practice for the sake of prestige and for spiritual advancement is attested in Augustine's congratulatory Letter 150 to Juliana and Proba on the occasion of Demetrias' conversion to asceticism. In that letter Augustine warns that many less exalted women will emulate Demetrias in order to associate themselves with her family's *claritas,* adding that if they wish to share in her renown they must also be encouraged to share in her holy manner of life.

So, too, the idea that women's yearning for the prestige of asceticism could spell disaster was not unknown to late fourth- and early fifth-century writers. Augustine's Letter 262 to Ecdicia, a married woman who had given away her son's inheritance without consulting the rest of the family, strikes a note of anxiety suspiciously like that of the would-be virgin's anxious relatives in the Apocryphal Acts.

To view the social tensions created in the aristocratic wing of the ascetic movement enables us to reframe the social-advancement question. In many respects, the question as it has been asked is misleading, since the definition of social advancement is so often an area of shifting terrain and since it presumes a continuity of social experience among women—despite differences in class or affiliation—for which there is no evidence.[34] This, in the end, is good news: by abandoning the generic category of "women's experience," we may at least be able to discern what we do know about the conditions for experience in various groups of women.

Asceticism seems to have made available to both women and men a wild card in the game of social ranking, a claim to elevated moral hygiene which could advance its bearer's standing in the group. This was no small benefit, as we can see in a number of texts that address married women's envy for the praise garnered by virgins. Certainly other wild cards existed: the success of a dancing girl such as the empress Theodora reminds us that in the vagaries of chance and favor some social mobility existed even in a system that prized stasis. Still, moral superiority was one of the few instruments by which women could attract positive attention to themselves. The performance of ascetic rigors served as an economical and reasonably decorous way to announce one's high moral standing.

Women of various classes found in the ascetic movement a social matrix by which they could dissociate themselves conclusively from the ancient equation of femininity and sexuality, particularly from its excessive antisocial, and repulsive aspect. Professional asexuality drew on the same rhetorical apparatus of feminine virtue by which some had long sought to mitigate negative accusations. The sexually active chastity of the senatorial *matrona*[35] would have been perceived as an eminently satisfactory vehicle for this rhetoric, but here class, not gender, was the obstacle. Few were born to such heights.

What singled out ascetic practice from other strategies for acquiring prestige was its accessibility. The social consequence to women of the rise of asceticism was not so much to offer new social prestige as it was to disrupt the traditional criteria for social ranking. Women as a group did not necessarily attain to new social prestige; rather, a different group of individual women was able to make social progress.

Here we begin to see an explanation for the link between the ascetic virgin and the chaste, self-effacing wife. Asceticism drew from the same rhetorical font as did the ideal of the chaste wife as guarantor of social

concord: both sought to dissociate particular women from the stereotype of the gender as persuaders to vice, while leaving unchallenged the
stereotype itself. In a social system based on competition among individuals and among families, to challenge such a stereotype would be in
no one's interest. Even if you feared the application of the stereotype
against yourself, you never knew when it might be useful against a rival.

Ascetic accomplishment was one area in which, although a woman's
standing was bound to modesty, she could nonetheless speak relatively
freely in her own favor. The traditional terms required a woman to
cultivate authority through a rhetoric of reluctance to personal power:
her authority might be great if she was wealthy and well-born, but it
was only respected where it was asserted in terms of *pietas,* that is, on
behalf of a shared value such as family, honor, or the common good.
This meant that a reputation for ascetic practice would have been an
asset especially useful to women. The rejection of worldly power implied
by the ascetic commitment might mean that a woman had to do less
rhetorical work to prove that her intentions were pious. And for the
woman whose worldly standing left something to be desired, asceticism
offered more practical advantages. Although the ideal of the chaste
Roman wife could be achieved fully only at the pinnacle of society,
asceticism made it possible for women to claim a prestige enhanced by
factors other than wealth or family status. Wealth and family prestige
could help, but they could be supplemented if lacking.

Finally, ascetic prestige was less vexed than traditional ideas of chaste
womanhood by failings in the woman's husband. (Even where a woman
could influence her parents' selection of a husband, she had little power
over the class status of the candidates.) To have a daughter marry well
in the late empire required sustained social campaigning, along with a
touch of good fortune—despite what you told your children, family
background was not always a sufficient indicator of future glory. The
uncertainty of the business would add to the cachet of those fortunate
enough to succeed, but it left a closed door to the unsuccessful. A
woman who married badly might be pitied, but rarely would she be
admired.

Asceticism, by contrast, seemed to offer some room for a woman to
choose her fate. Indeed, the literature of asceticism from its earliest
traces made it a virtue for a woman to have a husband or fiancé of

questionable character—her asceticism would then be all the more he-roic because of the obstacles posed—although the literature did in fact prefer that the bad man should come from an excellent family. The attraction of women to the ascetic ideal—and the alarm this attraction caused in some quarters—may perhaps be explained by this factor. If asceticism was perceived as allowing some women to dissociate their own status from that of their husbands or families, it would appeal to a broad spectrum of Roman women, for almost anyone might feel that her position could stand improvement.

Thus the appeal of the ascetic life can be explained in social terms. The status conferred by birth and marriage was an element of a woman's identity over which she could exert comparatively little control. Simi-larly, the traditional womanly virtues, such as *castitas,* could affect a woman's status only by enhancing her standing within her own group. Since these virtues were designed to stabilize rather than to disrupt the social order, their natural tendency was to work against social mobility. Yet the prestige of asceticism could confer something much like mo-bility in certain circumstances. Through the cultivation of ascetic virtue, a woman could aspire to participate in a network of social relationships by which she might be linked with others of a higher social standing on terms—those of Christian fellow feeling—that would compromise the distinctions of status. While this itself would not have conferred class mobility except in rare cases, the disruption of normative patterns of social interaction would benefit those whose ambition exceeded their reach within the traditional system.

Where class solidarity and the disposition of wealth were at stake, such disruptions might be dangerous to the social order. The *novellae* of Majorian, for example, record concern over the economic interests at stake in the decision of a widow to abandon custom and refuse re-marriage.[36] This suggests that her ability to invoke Christian piety as a pretext for disrupting the expected transmission of property, and the social fabric of which this pattern of transmission was a crucial element, was viewed as a threat to be stemmed by legislation if peer pressure did not work. The date of the legislation, twenty years before the nominal end of the western Roman empire, suggests that peer pressure had been unreliable.

Separatists and Traditionalists

We see, then, a division among Christians over the issue of cultural conservatism. What for some was and always had been a genuine search for identity was for others a pretext for self-righteousness: cultural allegiance became a rhetorically volatile issue as a separatist movement within Christianity emerged, whose proponents suggested that to value a heritage held in common with non-Christian friends and relatives was a matter of backsliding rather than of enlightened tolerance. Although the majority of literate Christians held the pagan literary and cultural heritage as unproblematic and something to be revered, accusations of paganism marshaled from earlier Christian writings were on the rise, even if they invoked a long-past moment when Christians had seen themselves as outsiders.

We should not mistake this separatism for moral authenticity, although that is precisely what its proponents intended. By creating confusion about the locus of moral authenticity, the proponents of cultural separatism were able to divest the Christian polity of the ideas of moderation and tolerance on which it had drawn over the centuries, in common with neighboring religious and philosophical systems. Instead, a fundamentalist language of intrinsic moral superiority was substituted.

A number of instances in the writings of Jerome mark this point. In his Letter 21 to Damasus, interpreting the story of the prodigal son, Jerome complains that "nowadays we see even priests of God—having abandoned the Gospels and the prophets—reading comedies, singing the erotic words of pastoral poems, sticking fast to Virgil, and making that crime, which in schoolboys is a matter of necessity, into a matter of choice" (13). This recalls Jerome's dream recounted to Eustochium in Letter 22, in which the climax of his progress in the wisdom of the desert is revealed as a repudiation of the wisdom of the schools:

> When many years ago for the sake of the kingdom of heaven I cut myself off from home, parents, sister, relations, and—what is even more difficult—from the habit of delicate foods, and made off for Jerusalem to fight the good fight, I was unable to do without the library which I had put together with great care when I was at Rome. And so, wretch that I was, I would fast knowing full well that I would read Cicero afterwards. After long nights of keeping vigil, after the

tears brought on by the memory of my past sins from my innermost heart, Plato would find his way into my hands. And if by chance, having returned to myself, I began to read one of the prophets, the inelegant language offended me, and because with blind eyes I did not see the light, I counted the failure to be that not of my own eyes but of the sun. (30)

The account continues in a similar vein until Jerome is taken sick with fever and preparations are made for his funeral. In his delirium, the young scholar receives a heavenly vision:

Suddenly in my mind I was carried away and dragged before the tribunal of the Judge, where the light was so great and the brightness shining from those who stood around so radiant, that having flung myself upon the ground I dared not look up. Asked to identify my estate, I replied that I was a Christian. But He who presided said, "You are lying: you are a Ciceronian, not a Christian. 'Where your treasure is, there also will be your heart' (Mt. 6.21)." (30)

Such accusations were less likely to emanate from the dais of the heavenly judge than from one's earthly rivals. While we will see Jerome accusing his former schoolmate Rufinus of being deceptively pagan, in his *Apology* Rufinus makes a similar charge against Jerome, and explicitly invokes Jerome's account of the "Ciceronian" dream to drive home his point.[37] Thus Rufinus was able to turn Jerome's seeming self-accusation against him in earnest.

What this means is that the question "Should Christians read pagan literature?" was highly artificial. In late fourth-century Rome, as Alan Cameron has shown, among the litterati "pagans" and "Christians" were first of all Romans. The more appropriate question would have been, "Are there circumstances under which it is to Christians' advantage to claim *not* to be reading pagan literature (even though they are)?" This question is more interesting and more complex, especially if what characterizes the outstanding Christian writers of the late fourth century is their relative cultural literacy. According to Cameron, although both Servius and Macrobius styled Virgil *pontifex maximus* and the *Aeneid* may have had a religious role in late paganism, this had no practical influence on the Christian use of Virgil, which was widespread.[38] In other words, for pragmatic reasons, a writer was likely to draw on a variety of authors across religious lines. The difficulty in pagan authors (for Christians) was not that they were pagan, or even that their writings had certain religious connotations; it was that these two facts could be used as *accusations* in certain circumstances.

An example of this phenomenon, again from Jerome, will bring us full circle. Writing to Ctesiphon around 413, Jerome attacks Rufinus' translation of the *Sentences of Sextus,* a volume that Rufinus had prepared in response to a request for a manual suitable for a prominent *matrona,* the niece of Melania the Elder.[39] The terms in which Jerome attacks Rufinus are revealing:

> Who could adequately describe the rashness or rather the crack-headedness of a fellow who ascribed the book of Sextus the Pythagorean (a man without Christ and a heathen!) to Xystus the martyr-bishop of the Roman church? In this book much is said of perfection in accordance with the doctrine of the Pythagoreans who make man equal to God and maintain that he is of God's substance; the result is that those who are ignorant that the volume is by a philosopher, supposing themselves to be reading the work of a martyr, drink of the golden cup of Babylon [cf. Jeremiah 51.7]. Furthermore, in that volume there is no mention of the prophets, of the patriarchs, of the apostles, and of Christ, so that he tries to make out that there was a bishop and a martyr who did not believe in Christ.[40]

It must be noted that Jerome himself was not (as one might imagine) condemning the Sextine maxims as a whole. Twenty years earlier, when his sights had been set not on Rufinus but on Jovinian, he had quoted with approbation one of the sayings: "The man who loves his wife quite passionately is himself an adulterer."[41] Even in his *Commentary on Ezekiel,* written in 417–419, around the same time as Letter 133, he cites the saying again with approval, but goes on to add: "A certain person translating that book into Latin, wanted to ennoble it by the name of the martyr Sixtus, not observing that in the entire volume (which he needlessly divided into two parts), the name of Christ and of the Apostles is entirely suppressed."[42]

Jerome is content with the sayings themselves, but the idea that a Pythagorean writing should be mistaken for the maxims of a martyr serves as an occasion for outrage and for denigrating the scholarly acumen of his onetime friend. When he characterizes those who read the maxims as "drinking of the golden cup of Babylon," the alarmist phrase is not so much a condemnation of the Sentences of Sextus as an opportunist move—Jerome uses an accusation of paganism as a pretext for insinuating that Rufinus cannot be trusted.

The role the *Sentences of Sextus* themselves played in the late fourth century merits discussion. Later we will encounter the phenomenon of philosophical literature addressed to *matronae* and the general trend to attribute to martyrs of the second and third century whatever one felt women needed to be told. For the moment, however, it is enough to bear in mind the paradox by which Christian writers were given to accusing one another of paganism, even as they themselves drew extensively on their Roman literary and philosophical training. We should not let the accusations blind us to this fact. On the subject of marriage, literate Christians drew on a variety of philosophical models, and we should remember to be surprised when they seem to neglect the terms and concerns of literate culture.

The contest between marriage and virginity electrified the dividing line between Christian traditionalists and Christian separatists. The separatists imputed to the traditionalists divided loyalties: any attempt to reinforce the established social order was seen as a betrayal of Christian authenticity for the sake of self-interest. To the traditionalists, however, there was nothing particularly authentic about the separatists. Whatever its original concern to enhance identity and participation among the faithful, the ascetic movement had become the means by which a self-righteous faction within the Christian polity took power at the expense of religious tolerance, a shared cultural heritage, and the social integration of pagans, Jews, and Christians.

· 5 ·

The Whispering Critics
at Blesilla's Funeral

"He was one of those men, and they are not the commonest, of whom we can know the best only by following them away from the market place, the platform, and the pulpit, entering with them into their own homes, hearing the voice with which they speak to the young and the aged about their own hearthstone, and witnessing their thoughtful care for the everyday wants of everyday companions, who take all their kindness as a matter of course, not as a subject for panegyric. Such men, happily, have lived in times when great abuses flourished, and have sometimes even been the living representatives of the abuses. That is a thought which might comfort us a little under the opposite fact—that it is better sometimes *not* to follow the great reformers of abuses beyond the threshold of their homes."[1]

Let the gentle irony of George Eliot's nineteenth-century narrator accompany us as we turn to the old-fashioned men and women of the fourth and fifth centuries who failed to secure a place in the ascetic movement. We know very little about them, which is understandable in view of their unpopularity with the monks and nuns responsible for transmitting historical sources from antiquity across the medieval period. What we do know about them is often presented in an unflattering light, captured for memory in the words of their opponents. And at times the archaeological finds that might correct the bias of our narrative sources seem only to confirm the ascetic critique of a church too comfortable in its imperial privileges.

To illustrate this point, we have only to think of one of the most famous objects preserved from the late fourth century, the silver casket given as a wedding gift to the young Christian heiress Proiecta, around 380, unearthed by workmen in 1793 at the foot of the Esquiline Hill in Rome and now held in the British Museum. The solid-silver case, nearly two feet long, seems to have been designed as a cosmetics box, a use suggested by its embossed and gilt figures of a nude Venus seated on a shell and attended by cupids. On the rim of the lid are two inscriptions. One, "Secundus and Proiecta, live in Christ!" commemorates the marriage even as it contravenes the presence of the unavoidably pagan Venus. The second inscription is more compromising: "Twenty-two pounds, three-and-a-half ounces."[2]

It takes an act of imagination not to assume that the donor of the Proiecta casket had a poor grasp of what it meant to "live in Christ." But just such an act of imagination is required if we wish to read behind the triumphalism of the late fourth-century ascetic party. The city's urgent need for concord among its ruling members had been vested since the time of Augustus in the image of Venus, goddess of love and patroness of marriage.[3] The distinction here is not really between authentic and compromised models of Christianity—it is between two very different conceptions of the body social. One, the separatist view, sees religious ideals as a means of distinguishing the chosen few from the unenlightened masses. The other, the civic view, sees these ideals as including and uniting the whole of society under the aegis of divine protection.[4] The historical success of the separatist view should not blind us to the integrity of the civic view of religion among late Roman Christians. We will see that their defense of marriage was central to their defense of the communal ordering of life, which the ascetics disparagingly referred to as the *saeculum*, the world.

Civic Ideals of Marriage

If we can believe Jerome, these men and women thought of men like him as "detestable monks."[5] To find out why we must explore sources to which little attention has been paid in discussing the rise of asceticism. These are sources less rhetorically expansive than the treatises designed to defend or promote asceticism; in part, this is because sustained arguments against asceticism, such as the writings of Jerome's adversary Jovinian, were eventually condemned by the Church and were not kept safe by the monastic libraries to which we owe the preservation of our ancient texts. So we must glean an idea of the defense of marriage from oblique and telegraphic sources. Still, because the ancient divide between public and private was drawn rather differently from our own, there are moments when we may follow men and women into their homes, and even into the marriage chamber, by means of sources so public and conventional as to have seemed unexceptional to the ancient eye even if they are revealing to ours.

To understand the traditional ideals of which marriage stood as an emblem, we may begin in the schoolroom. A late fourth-century school manual of rhetoric, the *Progymnasmata* of Aphthonius of Antioch, is interesting precisely because it represents a late fourth-century notion of "what went without saying" on the subject of marriage. Aphthonius begins his advice on how an orator should argue a thesis by breaking the problem down into subcategories according to the kind of thesis to be argued. The two subcategories are reassuringly, typically classical. The thesis can either be political or speculative. "The political are those which are concerned with the problems affecting a city, for example, whether one should marry . . . or build fortifications, for these things affect a city." The speculative thesis considers matters such as whether the sky is spherical or whether there are many worlds: "These do not originate within the experience of man, and they are considered in the mind alone." Characteristically ancient about this opposition is the assumption that human beings can only come into discussion insofar as they are relevant to "the problems affecting a city."

When he turns to illustrate how a political thesis should be argued, Aphthonius gives as an example the question whether a man should marry. As he argues it, the good of marriage for the city is in the way it ties men to common purpose through shared self-interest:

> First of all, [marriage] stirs men to bravery . . . since marriage knows how to produce the children and wives over whom war is fought . . . it provides righteous men along with the brave . . . since men who are

anxious about the things in which posterity takes pride do those things justly . . . Nay more, it makes men wise whom it inspires to provide for [their] dearest ones.

In addition, marriage leads men to a cultivation of the virtues of self-control on which the reliable conduct of the citizen is based.

> And by way of paradox, marriage knows how to supply self-control, and moderation is mingled with pursuit of the pleasures . . . since it adds convention to the pleasures, marriage supplies moderate pleasures in support of its convention, and the arraigning of the one with the other within marriage is to be marvelled at.

Thus, Aphthonius concludes triumphantly, marriage is an irreproachable school of virtue for the citizen: "Accordingly, to the extent that marriage . . . provides brave and just men at the same time, and if it furnishes wise and temperate men, how is it possible not to hold marriage in high esteem?"[6]

For our purposes, it is interesting to see the question treated as one whose answer is self-evident, given the fact that Aphthonius was writing just as marriage as a founding civic virtue was coming under attack, in part because the city itself was increasingly an object of derision. Aphthonius was a student of Libanius and thus, rhetorically speaking, a foster brother of John Chrysostom, who despite his edifying sermons on Christian marriage was a fierce proponent of the virtues of the desert and virginity. When we consider that he was also a close contemporary on the Latin side of Jerome, who wrote so vituperatively against marriage, it is surprising to remember that at the time it was Aphthonius who was still in the majority.

Franca Ela Consolino has suggested that in the late fourth century pagans and Christians were divided over the question of married women, since Christianity did not allow the same ritual prominence to married women as did pagan cults.[7] This is an important point, but there is no real reason to assume that such an opposition would have been constituted along the lines of religious affiliation, with uniform views within either group. Traditionalist Christians would have held in common with their pagan friends and relatives the ideology of marriage as a civic partnership that had prevailed for centuries.

One reason that scholars have underestimated this common ground may be the tendency of Christian writers to accuse one another of consorting with pagan ideas and literature, as we have seen. Another reason may be quite simply that scholars have tended to overestimate the degree to which Jerome's sanctimonious posturing was approved by his contemporaries. (We will see below that even his allies found it necessary to censor his zeal.)

Further, we often forget that Christianity was not the only religious movement attracting enthusiastic converts and the apprehension of traditionalists. David Hunter has shown that, from the 380s on, ascetic writers were increasingly anxious to dissociate themselves from the lively Manichaean contingent at Rome. The distinction became all the more important since the Manichaeans' claims to moral superiority were very similar to those of orthodox ascetics, with the stress in each case on virginity and fasting. Hunter has shown concretely that authors such as Jerome (and Augustine later during his battle with Julian of Eclanum) had to be concerned that their own attempts to promote asceticism should not be interpreted as pro-Manichaean.

According to Hunter, Augustine's letter to the Manichee Secundinus (dated between 390 and 410) indicates that Secundinus denigrated the Old Testament patriarchs on the grounds that they married: their need to marry signaled their lack of virtue and the inferiority of the Hebrew Bible.[8] This helps to explain the positions of Jovinian and Helvidius, two antiascetic Christian writers whose work we know only through Jerome's sardonic responses to their work. Jovinian, affirming the virtue of the patriarchs, seems to have insinuated that to exalt virginity over marriage was a denigration of the Hebrew Bible; Helvidius suggested that it did no dishonor to the Virgin Mary for Christians to recognize that she had been a wife to Joseph and a mother to children other than Jesus, because to be a spouse and parent was in accord with the role of the Hebrew patriarchs.[9] The implied argument of both authors is an expostulation: surely celibates were not suggesting that their vocation was superior to that of the Hebrew patriarchs!

Jerome's response to Jovinian and Helvidius—and to a third, Vigilantius, whose visit to Jerome at Bethlehem had resulted in a sustained attack on monasticism, the cult of relics, and holy-land pilgrimage—was ferocious. It is his *Against Jovinian* (c. 393) that constitutes his most sustained argument and drew most criticism from his contemporaries. The text is organized along the lines of a standard rhetorical exercise, a reverse version of the argument "whether a man should marry" sketched out by Aphthonius of Antioch. The treatise draws heavily on the "cares of marriage," a standard topos from Hellenistic and Roman versions of the argument.[10]

Jerome was chastened by the chilling reception to his treatise. Augustine's criticism was covert but devastating: where Jerome had asserted that it was Christian virgins who were the true heirs of the *matronae* of antiquity whom Romans male and female had studied as exemplars of singular virtue, Augustine offered up a treatise *On the Good of Marriage* and another *On Holy Virginity* (both c. 400–401), which explicitly warned virgins that to cultivate a sense of implicit superiority to the married would be at best a mistake and at worst the occasion of their own spiritual downfall.[11] Jerome's Letter 49 to Pammachius represents an attempt to soften the ferocity of his attack on Jovinian. He asserts that despite his sardonic comments on Jovinian's position and on the married more generally, his intention was not to condemn marriage itself but rather to outline a middle way between the Jewish and pagan affirmation of marriage and the Manichaean rejection. Further, he states in his defense that in composing the treatise he was writing *gymnastikōs* (to confute) and not *dogmatikōs* (to instruct).[12] This anxiety over genre is extremely important. We can see in the exchange between Jerome and Pammachius a concern about how the debate over marriage and asceticism—a nasty business of power relations among specialists— should be tempered before reaching the general, and perhaps especially the female, public. Jerome himself had stated in his Letter 22 to Eustochium that while he exalted virginity, and urged her toward *sancta superbia* (holy arrogance) because of her own practice of it (16), she should not understand him as condemning marriage out of hand (19).

"The Fellowship of a Lifetime"

At the same time, traditionalists both pagan and Christian were elaborating the ideal of marriage in increasingly spiritualized language. We see this clearly in contemporary funerary inscriptions. Perhaps most moving is the series of inscriptions still preserved on a stele in the Palazzo dei Conservatori at Rome, commemorating a pagan couple, Vettius Agorius Praetextatus and Fabia Aconia Paulina, and describing their shared life.[13] Praetextatus has long been recognized as the central heroic figure of the pagan resistance within the late fourth-century Senate and indeed as "the exemplar of late senatorial paganism."[14] Praetorian prefect and consul-designate for the following year at the time of his death in late 384, Praetextatus stood at the pinnacle of the Roman political hierarchy, and the partnership of Paulina, it is clear, graced his tenure visibly and publicly.

The stele itself, inscribed on all four sides, seems to have been erected by Paulina early in her widowhood. The front bears the *cursus honorum* of Praetextatus and the religious initiations of Paulina in the customary telegraphic style, concluding with the simple statement that "these two lived together for forty years" (*ILS* 1259, B3). On each side of the stele is a brief poem dedicated to Paulina by Praetextatus, and on the back a long poem to Praetextatus from Paulina.

The language of the poems to Paulina stresses both public and private aspects of her virtue—and the link between the two. In the poem on the right face of the stele, the assimilation of civic to conjugal *pietas*—"putting forward her husband before herself, and Rome before the man"—is explicit. The poem on the left face is worth quoting in full:

> Paulina, partner of my heart, spark of modesty, bond of chastity, pure love and faith sprung forth from heaven, to whom I have entrusted the revealed secrets of my heart, gift of the gods who entwine our marriage-bed with amicable and decorous bonds, by the *pietas* of a mother, the charm of a wife, the duty of a sister, the unassuming conduct of a daughter, and by how great a trust are we joined to one another in amity, by the fellowship of a lifetime, by the pact of consecration, by a faithful yoke and open-hearted concord; delighting your husband, loving, adorning, cherishing.[15]

The language here is both touching and highly traditional. The "amicable and decorous bonds" of family life are revealed in a kaleidoscope of Paulina's alternating identities within the family unit; we may be surprised to see Paulina remembered as a daughter in the context of her own marriage until we remember that her father, Aconius Catullinus, was himself prefect and *consul ordinarius*.

The lengthy inscription framed as Paulina's speech to Praetextatus on the back of the stele offers a much more detailed glimpse of their religious life. She begins with an account of his scholarly activity—he

seems to have been expert in the correction of Greek and Latin philosophical manuscripts, an activity vital to a manuscript-based literary
culture, and one that pagans and many learned Christians held to be
an important stage in the preparation of the soul for mystical experience.[16] Paulina refers to the ancient authors whom Praetextatus had
studied as "the wise, to whom the gate of heaven is open," a point that
occasioned fierce criticism from some Christian authors even as much
of the language and imagery of the poem was shared by her counterparts
among the Christian *matronae*.

At the end of the inscription, we hear Paulina speaking directly to
her husband:

> You, husband, deliver me pure and chaste from the lot of death by
> the goodness of your teaching, lead me into the temples and dedicate
> me to the gods as their handmaid. With you as witness I am initiated
> into all the mysteries. You, in your duty as a husband, consecrate me
> as priestess of Didymenes and Attis through the rites of the bull. You
> instruct me, as priestess of Hecate, in the threefold secrets and you
> prepare me for being worthy of the rites of Greek Ceres ... Now,
> robbed of all this I, your grief-stricken wife, waste away. Happy would
> I have been had the gods granted that my husband had outlived me.
> Yet I am happy because I am yours, was yours, and soon—after
> death—shall be yours. (*ILS* 1259, D22–29; 38ff)

The voice of the widowed Paulina is to a modern ear vivid and compelling in its affection and grief, and yet we should not forget that the
language in which she mourns her husband has a public aspect as well.
Paulina's account of shared religious experience complements Praetextatus' *cursus honorum* and confers on it the dignity of lived and felt
experience. The civic and priestly accomplishments of both spouses
were enhanced by their conjugal unity, and their shared *pietas* would
have been perceived as no less profound and moving—rather more so—
for its decorous public aspect.

We can gather only the faintest trace of the network of relationships
in which Paulina participated through her many initiations and offices.
An inscription found on the Esquiline Hill, in the area where Paulina's
and Praetextatus' house is believed to have stood, records her gratitude
to the chief Vestal virgin, who had erected a statue in tribute to Praetextatus after his death:

> To Coelia Concordia, chief among the Vestal Virgins. Fabia Paulina, c[larissima] f[emina], commissioned this statue to be made and erected, not only on account of her singular modesty and her extraordinary piety toward the sacred cult, but also because she had erected a statue to her [Paulina's] husband Vettius Agorius Praetextatus, v[ir] c[larissimus], outstanding in everything and likewise worthy to be revered by the virgins and priests of this order. (*ILS* 1261)

Praetextatus had been high priest of the Vestals during his lifetime, and the exchange of statues between Coelia Concordia and Paulina hints at the tie of shared piety between the virgin and the married woman. We know from a letter of Praetextatus' close associate, Quintus Aurelius Symmachus, that the cult-governing college of *pontifices* (of which he was a member) had approved the erection of the statue, although some were concerned that for the virgins to make such a gesture independently of the Senate would contravene tradition. Symmachus records his own endorsement of that view, adding "yet I kept quiet, lest something repeated to rivals of the cult cause offense to those proposing the innovation."[17] Coelia Concordia was perceived as a religious innovator, which suggests that the threat posed by Christianity during those years may well have divided the senatorial class. Some, even in a traditionalist order like the Vestal virgins, opted for religious experimentation while others feared that any breach of tradition would play into the hands of the Christians.

But when the outward signs of Paulina's spiritual union with her revered husband attracted blame, it was from an entirely different quarter. By chance, one of Jerome's letters preserves a vituperative reference to what seems to be Paulina's poem to Praetextatus. Soon after Praetextatus' death in 384, Jerome writes in Letter 23 to Marcella:

> O, what a great reversal of fortune! He whom the heights of all honors preceded (only a few days before), who ascended the Capitoline as if proceeding in triumph over enemies cast down, whom the Roman people received with applause and dancing, by whose death the universal city was shaken—now he is abandoned, naked, not in the milk-white palace of heaven, as his unhappy wife suggests, but imprisoned in the foul darkness. (3)

We can hear Jerome attempting to win Marcella away from an allegiance with a member of the senatorial aristocracy to whom she would by tradition owe a much greater loyalty than she did to Jerome and his kind. By construing Paulina's reference to the gate of heaven in hyperbolic terms—placing Praetextatus himself in "the milk-white palace of heaven"—he mocks not only a religious competitor but, as it happens, a man appointed to the highest office of a Roman political career.

Jerome's attack on marriage as a necessary evil and his attack on Paulina may have been linked. Perhaps the civic prestige that Paulina, as commissioner of the epitaph, was able to assert for her position as priestess in her own right and partner of the great Praetextatus provoked Jerome's ire precisely because one of the attractions of Christian asceticism was its emphasis on female spiritual advancement and religious activity.[18] Certainly the spiritualized image of the conjugal bond would have upset a writer like Jerome, if he meant to persuade aristocratic ladies to eschew a marriage such as Paulina's. There is no reason, however, to assume that Jerome's ascetic views (or his sardonic attitude) would have been considered normative among Christians. The instinctive response of someone like Marcella may well have been a distaste for Jerome's vulgarity.

Still Jerome was not alone in his hostility to Praetextatus, Paulina, and their kind. It has been suggested that the anonymous turn-of-fifth-century Latin poem known as the *Carmen contra paganos* was intended as an attack on the pair.[19] The poem's imaginative setting is the city of Rome, after the death of a universally beloved prefect. A great deal of ink has been spilled over the identity of the prefect at the center of the poem's satire, but for our purposes it is unnecessary to resolve the problem conclusively. Beginning from the view that the Praetextatus stele outlines an ideal of the conjugal relationship whose religious overtones would have been acknowledged by other men and women of the senatorial class, we can discern in the *Carmen* a response to this genre of praise for the married dead, if not a response to this very inscription.

It was not a pretty response. The poem is crude in its language and manner of presentation, and seems intent on eliciting revulsion for the dead prefect. The opening lines of the poem attack a group of senators in terms that almost immediately begin to draw on images of sexual impurity and sexual excess, precisely the social violations against which marriage would ideally protect the public man. Then the poem moves from satirizing public figures to slurs against the gods themselves, "incestuous . . . the sister married to her brother" (line 4). A thirteen-line invective against Jupiter, father of the gods, follows. If we remember the affectionate description by Achilles Tatius of a mural of Zeus and Europa, we will be surprised by the tone of disgust. The emphasis here is on lustful excess, adultery, and bestiality: "This Jupiter of yours . . . overcome by love of Leda . . . would bellow as an adulterous bull? If these monstrosities are found pleasing, nothing holy is undefiled."[20]

When the main object of the poem's satire, a deceased prefect resembling Praetextatus, is introduced in line 25, the reason for the debasement of Jupiter becomes evident: "The Christian opinion, that not even the agonized death of the *praefectus* was adequate repayment for his wickedness, is contrasted with the delusion of pagans, that their champion had after his death been 'seized' to the throne of Jupiter—that is, to heaven."[21] According to the logic of the poem, the fate of the prefect who falsely believed he would reach the throne of Jupiter is doubly hideous if Jupiter himself is understood not as sacred but as profane. The reference to the prefect's disputed fate after death reminds us of Jerome's Letter 23, in which the great pagan was condemned to "foul darkness." In lines 87–88, the *Carmen* asks him, "What was Paphian Venus, and Juno Pronuba, and the old man Saturn, able to do for you as an initiate?" Among the list of gods whose powers are ridiculed in this passage, the inclusion of Paphian Venus and Juno *pronuba*—that is, in her capacity as patron goddess of marriage—is appropriate.

Finally, the last eight lines of the poem (115–122) seem directly to echo Paulina's inscription (or another in the same genre), a fact that has not to my knowledge been taken into account in the debate over the identity of the prefect excoriated in the *Carmen*. These lines may be quoted in full:

All of those monstrosities which you worshipped, stationed in the temple, your wife, a suppliant with spelt-offerings and [praying hands], while she heaps the altars with gifts and prepares to fulfill her vows to the gods and goddesses at the threshold of the shrine, and threatens the gods, wishing by magic spells to sway Acheron, sent the wretch headlong to Tartarus below. Give up mourning for such a dropsical spouse, who wanted to hope for salvation from Latian Jupiter.

The image of the suppliant wife at the altar threatening the gods and intoning magical spells seems a rough parody of Paulina's "You, husband, deliver me pure and chaste from the lot of death" (lines 22–24).

Similarly, the poem's closing thought—"Give up mourning for such a dropsical spouse!"—seems apt as a grotesque rejoinder to Paulina's poem, which turns from a chronicle of Praetextatus' accomplishments to the plangent "Now, robbed of all this, I, your grief-stricken wife, waste away. Happy would I have been had the gods granted that my husband had outlived me" (lines 38–40). While Paulina is concerned to maintain a sense of decorum, of resolution and proper order (the phrase just quoted continues "Yet I am happy because I am yours, was yours, and soon—after death—shall be yours," to end the poem), the *Carmen* seems intent in its treatment of the grieving widow to show that all is as far from order and decorum as is humanly imaginable. This would have been particularly appropriate if the *Carmen* was directed at humiliating a couple who were publicly annointed as an exemplum of dignity, moderation, and decency; the final scene gives added resonance to the theme of lustful excess that attaches to the prefect throughout the poem.

It is the obsessive interest of the *Carmen* in producing an effect of revulsion that ought to hold our attention. We should not be tempted to an easy acceptance of Jerome and the *Carmen contra paganos* as representative witnesses to Christian thinking on the subject. Rather, I would argue, the fact that these two sources are so strident in their disrespect for a prefect's grief-stricken widow is in itself significant. Such stridency cannot safely be identified as a characteristic Christian response to paganism—rather, it needs to be understood as a controversial statement of the Christian position, and one that not all Christians would acknowledge. After all, the Christian prefects and consuls had their widows too. In this case, as perhaps in others, Jerome's invective must have seemed to moderate Christians to be verging on the kind of perversity that the *Carmen* exemplified.[22]

This point can be illustrated by the epitaph of the Christian Sextus Petronius Probus (grandfather of Anicia Demetrias), who died some time after 388. The inscription, from his mausoleum at St. Peter's, mingles the shared language of late antiquity with the specific language of the Christian faith: "you safely run your course over the expanse of the heavens untouched by vice; like your name in probity your fame resounds in your character too; washed clean in the Jordan you are now Probus [upright] better than before."[23] More significant for our purposes is the ending. Here we see the Christian widow Proba evoked according to the same conventions as her pagan contemporary Paulina had followed:

> Far be it from you, Rome, to believe that your Probus should have died for such services as his; he lives and possesses the stars; friend of virtue, faith, duty, and honor; not sparing of his riches to any man and prodigal of himself. Nevertheless, Proba, the best of wives, obtained this solace for so great a grief as hers, that the urn unites them as equals. Happy, alas too happy, was she, joined to so worthy a man while alive, and worthy of the same tomb. (*CIL* 6.1756)

Another dedication, this time to the widow Proba by her sons, echoes the poem to Paulina in its definition of the honor and in terms of her family relationships:

> To Anicia Faltonia Proba, adorning the Amnii, the Pincii, and the Anicii; a consul's wife, a consul's daughter, and mother of consuls; Anicius Probinus, v[ir] c[larissimus], consul ordinarius, and Anicius Probus, v[ir] c[larissimus], quaestor candidatus, sons beholden to a mother's merits, dedicated [this]. (*ILS* 1269, 5ff)

Thus, rather than a characteristically Christian attack on idealized Roman marriage, Jerome and the *Carmen contra paganos* should be seen as striving to undermine a civic tradition close to the hearts of *both* Christians and pagans of the ruling class. Each can be—and would have been—read as creating revulsion against the repository of values for a shared culture in matters of moderation and decorum. If modern scholars imagine that this distaste for the civic tradition was common to all Christians, it is only because of the success of its proponents in shaping the transmission of historical memory.

Advice to Married Women

It is in this context that we should understand Rufinus of Aquileia's decision to translate the *Sentences of Sextus* into Latin, which Jerome criticized as the result of "crack-headedness." The translation was dedicated to the married couple Avita and Apronianus. We know something about the family of each. Avita was the niece of Melania the elder and a cousin once removed of Melania the younger, whose fame and ascetic reputation we have already seen. Her husband, Turcius Apronianus, may have been a first cousin to the Turcius Secundus whose wife Proiecta was given the famous silver casket.[24]

The translation of the *Sentences* seems to have been part of a wider attempt by Rufinus to put at the disposal of the literate Christian laity a devotional literature that would impart a sense of Christian purpose and identity to those whose lives the ascetic movement had not entirely rearranged. Thus we have his translation of Origen's *Commentary on St. Paul's Epistle to the Romans* and the anonymous family romance of the *Pseudo-Clementine Recognitions;* the preface to his translation of Origen's *Homilies on Psalms 36–38,* dedicated to Apronianus, mentions that he has had the sermons bound in a single volume to serve as a convenient manual of spiritual formation.[25] Avita appears in this preface as someone who is reassured that "such matters are not beyond the depth of feminine competence";[26] it closes with the reassurance that "the human body could not be only sinews and bones, if the divine providence had not interwoven it with the softness of flesh, and the comforts of plumpness."

It is the *Sentences of Sextus,* however, which is directed specifically to Avita, the Christian *matrona.* Rufinus' preface to his translation hands on the tradition that Sextus was in fact the Roman pope-martyr Xystus (Sixtus). He claims for the martyr's dicta a purity of speech and a power of meaning that later emerged as criteria of ascetic achievement:

> This man, once she has read him, she will find so brief that she will see single lines enfold vast meanings, so powerful that the saying of a single line may suffice for the perfecting of a whole life, so plain-spoken that a girl whose mind is distracted may not give as an excuse to her reader that she is unable to follow the meaning.[27]

Like the homilies of Origen bound together as a manual for her husband, the dicta in their brevity were intended to serve as a constant point of reference.

> The entire work is so brief, that it is possible for the whole book never to leave her hands, attaining the place of a certain person's single,

precious, ring. And in truth it seems fair that someone to whom for the sake of the word of God earthly ornaments have revealed themselves as of small account, should now instead be adorned by us with the necklaces of the Word and of wisdom.

The metaphor of the ring—a play on the literal meaning of the Greek *encheiridion,* the book's title—reinforces the idea that the work should be kept close at hand: "Now, then, let her have in her hands for a while this book in the place of a ring, and after a time, let it be preserved in her memory as a treasury of the whole discipline of good actions, ready to afford admonitions from its hidden innermost recesses." Like Proiecta's silver casket, the Latin translation of the *Sentences of Sextus* is an exhortation to "live in Christ" within the language of feminine charm and adornment.

There is no reason to believe that, because Rufinus refers to Avita when addressing Apronianus in both prefaces as "your sister in Christ," the marriage between the two had been pledged to continence. The reasons for furnishing a fertile, chaste *matrona* with edifying readings would have been sound, for the *matronae* had begun to notice that their status as exemplars of virtue was on the wane. This may explain the division between polemical position and pastoral instinct which Jerome referred to in his letter to Pammachius. We see the phenomenon in other writers, perhaps most clearly in Augustine and Pelagius, men whose disagreement over free will and grace eventually developed into a debate on marriage and concupiscence replete with accusations of Manichaeism.[28] Yet where practical advice to married women was concerned, the Augustinian and Pelagian positions were difficult to distinguish. Since the dating of the following letters is uncertain, the similarity of their views might be explained away on chronological grounds, by the idea that the debate had not yet polarized by the time the letters were written. But on pastoral issues addressed directly to women, the distance may never have been very great.

Augustine's letter to Ecdicia and the letter to Celantia now attributed to Pelagius[29] share a situation in which a woman has of her own accord and without her husband's consent made a vow of chastity, and her repudiation of conjugal relations is claimed by the husband as a pretext for adultery. Anxiety over the social consequences of the ascetic movement comes through as a vital force behind the writing in both letters.

Augustine opens by saying he is sorry that Ecdicia has behaved in such a way as to besmirch the cause of continence with the ruin of adultery. He goes on to warn her that he knows her vow was unilateral and therefore illegal, a crime not because continence itself attains no merit but as a fundamental violation of marital *consensus*. Fortunately, after the fact Ecdicia did obtain a grudging consent from her husband, and thus whether she should return to him, given the unilateral nature of the initial vow, is not in question.[30] Thus Augustine is spared the difficult question of adjudicating between a vow of continence and a vow of marriage. Which would have been more important—concord between spouses or continence—if they had to be set in opposition? One imagines that in the pastoral advising of families during this period, such problems must have arisen.[31] The claims of continence could work havoc on a senatorial dynasty, as we know from the case of Melania and Pinian.

In the case of Pelagius' letter to Celantia, which bears close affinities to his letter to Demetrias and seems therefore to belong to the mid teens of the fifth century,[32] the situation is slightly different. Celantia is in precisely the difficult spot that Ecdicia had managed to avoid. Having committed herself to continence without her husband's consent, she must now abrogate either 1 Corinthians 7.5 ("Defraud ye not one another") or her vow of continence (30). In each case it is clear that the writer, whatever his own sense of the value of the woman's ascetic ideals, felt that he could not be seen to encourage her in repudiating her marital vows.

There was another factor at play: at the time of Ecdicia's vow of continence, she had given away her inheritance to wandering monks without consulting either her husband or her son, her prospective heir. It is not clear how much money was involved, but it was enough to cause serious commotion when the deed was discovered. Augustine does not dispute her right to dispose of her own money as she sees fit, but he is worried about the repercussions within the family of such an aggressive gesture against her son's expectations. We know nothing—and it is of course possible that Augustine knew nothing—about the monks to whom Ecdicia donated her wealth. It is somewhat surprising that Augustine does not take a tone of censure against them. The possibilities of disorder would have been endless if men and women in unhappy marriages were encouraged to distribute their property to any ascetic who happened along, without consulting their spouses—especially, as Augustine notes here, where there were children who might themselves grow up to have family obligations despite a parent's fit of ascetic zeal.

A Manual for *Matronae*

This may have been the concern behind the writing of the *Liber ad Gregoriam*, an anonymous devotional manual addressed to a Latin-speaking *matrona* in the imperial household who may or may not have been Gregoria, *cubicularia augustae* in Constantinople at the end of the sixth century.[33] It is indicative of the little attention paid until recently to the construction of gender and female religious identity in late antiquity that this treatise, unique for its period in addressing the religious and ethical concerns of a married Christian laywoman, has not been the subject of sustained scholarly inquiry.[34]

Robert Markus calls the *Liber* a "mirror for wives,"[35] which is as fair a description as any of its elusive form. We see a similar characterization of the text by one of its few attested medieval readers: the explicit of a ninth-century manuscript of the *Liber* preserved at Reichenau records it as a *de officiis matronalibus,* a manual of duties for *matronae.*[36] The genre *de officiis matronalibus* is otherwise unattested in antiquity, but it seems an apt description, since the *Liber* shares with Cicero's *De officiis* (On Duties) and with works such as the *De officiis* of Ambrose or the *Pastoral Rule* of Gregory the Great a systematic approach to the particular responsibilities of a given estate, in this case that of the Roman *matrona.*

In the known manuscripts, this unusual treatise is divided into twenty-five chapters, which proceed in miscellaneous fashion through the various practical, devotional, and theoretical issues that a married woman of some standing might encounter. The treatment of servants, for example, receives attention commensurate with that accorded to the justification of the married estate or the exhortation to daily martyrdom.

The preface depicts "Gregoria" as having requested "a ruling on what place a wife will be able to find before God," a request the author interprets as an invitation to elaborate a full-fledged spirituality for the married estate. The central proposal of the initial section of the text is that the married must interpret their estate both as an emblem of the instability of the *saeculum* and as a beneficial tempering at the hands of the Deity. A dense sequence of biblical quotations[37] in chapter 1 establishes that the trials of married life are to be seen as a medium through which the virtue of endurance—*patientia*—may be cultivated.

The overarching metaphor of the *Liber* is the *conflictus*, the battle between the vices and the virtues, a metaphor that casts the *matrona* as the object of a cosmic struggle between God and "the Enemy of the Human Race."[38] The metaphor relies on the addressee's pose of reluctance: though she is married, and fulfills her duties within the family, she does so only with modest regret for the higher things from which she is diverted. Chapter 2 calls her to battle, exhorting her to defend the nobility not of the body but of the soul. This representation of the battle of vices and virtues is designed to help her remember that the irritations of the sublunary are useful to hone the steel of spiritual discernment.

Chapters 3 and 4 are an excursus on endurance as the virtue par excellence for the married, who are vulnerable to misinterpretation by the ignorant of their humility in choosing such a little-exalted estate. They should count any injustice they may suffer as an opportunity to reflect on the humiliations to which Christ was subjected. Chapter 5 takes up the problem of endurance in a colorful, hectoring tone, mocking the *matrona*'s sincerity in wishing to imitate the martyrs, if she is afraid of the lesser trials of marriage. A band of married martyrs (Symphorosa, Felicitas of Rome, Anastasia, and Hannah, the mother of the Maccabees) is introduced, who confirm that the endurance required in married life is the same stuff as that of glorious martyrdom.

Chapters 6–9 discuss the conduct of a wife toward her husband. Here the stress is on the idea that while a husband may initially be perceived as an obstacle to the spiritual life, his troublesome presence should in fact be seen as an opportunity for feats of spiritual heroism. The rule that a wife must be seen to obey the will of her husband is cast as an invitation to display the magnetic quality of her own inclination toward the spiritual, with the result that "he may cease to keep his own counsel, and will receive your whole will as a divine pattern, and shiver at your displeasure as at sacrilege" (7).

This outline of the trials and opportunities that a married Christian woman might have to face is interrupted at chapter 10 by an allegorical excursus. The *matrona* is invited to ascend the "tower of contemplation,"[39] thence to witness the battle between the *miles Christi* and a succession of personified vices (chapters 11–15). The scene is reported simultaneously as a *conflictus,* an actual battle account, and as an *altercatio,* a debate in dialogue form between the soldier of Christ and the successive vices (falsehood, avarice, faithlessness, gluttony, and desire of the flesh).

The excursus has the flavor of a monastic manual, and the fact that it is addressed in the first-person singular masculine suggests the possibility that it is (or is intended to be taken for) a segment borrowed from a work of ascetic instruction originally intended for men. Such borrowings had become a commonplace of devotional literature by the end of the sixth century, and one would be plausible here. The *Liber* certainly knows other borrowings, such as a paraphrase in chapter 16 of chapter 15 of Tertullian's *On Patience* and a miracle story in chapter 8 that shares characteristics with the lives of the desert fathers. If the excursus is a borrowing, its source has yet to be recovered, but there may have been compelling literary reasons for its invention.

Chapter 16 resumes the discussion of the virtue of endurance in the life of the Christian *matrona.* Chapter 17 treats the question of dutiful conduct toward the husband, linking it to the biblical themes of searching out the will of God and keeping his mandates,[40] themes of enduring interest to devotional writers, especially in the wake of the sermons and letters of John Chrysostom and the Pelagians at the beginning of the fifth century.

It is in chapters 18 and 19 that the *de officiis* genre finds more conventional exposition, with advice on the governance of the household, the *matrona*'s traditional activity of weaving and spinning, and the cultivation of personal conduct as an exemplum for lesser members of the household. The importance of reputation and the choice of respectable associates is also discussed, as is the question of justice in the treatment of slaves.

Another text, a brief, untitled treatise on the governance of the household addressed to a Christian *matrona* in the early fifth century, attests that the managerial responsibilities of the aristocratic household were themselves being Christianized, in the sense that spiritual meaning was explicitly assigned to the peaceable exercise of authority over one's subordinates and to forbearance in interpersonal relationships more generally.[41]

Returning to the *Liber,* the advice on slaves raises the issue of God's own justice, which is the theme of the last section of the treatise. Chapters 20 and 21 serve as a warning that, while instinctively she may defend her nobility in earthly terms, the Christian woman should take care "to protect the nobility of the soul," lest God's justice turn against her. Chapters 22 to 24 review the requirements of the Christian life and stress the urgency of safeguarding the divine precepts by assiduous "searching and observance" (24). To the objection that it is not the place of the married to excel in the Christian life, our author replies that the *caritas* of marriage is itself a vehicle of grace.

Chapter 25 of the *Liber,* the final one, draws together these threads into an *ascensus,* wherein the reader finds herself again lifted up, but this time, instead of being encouraged to look down on the battlefield of this life, she is directed to fix her gaze firmly toward the gate of heaven. This has been the object of the study of the will of God, "for in this door [the study of God's will] heaven is either closed or lies open to us." The daily progress in virtue is figured now as a pressing toward the summit of the mountain path that leads to heaven: "as we progress, let us avert our eyes entirely from below, lest, shaken by a vertiginous fear of height while we look down, we should tumble down into the lower depths from the very heights of heaven, cast headlong by the whirling." Such a visionary ascent belongs to the world of ascetic technique—as in the late sixth-century *Moralia in Job* of Gregory the Great—but it is equally at home in the world of civic religion, as we have seen in the epitaph of Petronius Probus.

The problem addressed by the *Liber ad Gregoriam* is, fundamentally, how to reinvent civic religion in the image of asceticism. To accommodate the experience of *matronae* within Christian moral language in light of the ascetic takeover, this seemed a promising method. But the ascetic ideal had also absorbed aspects of the legacy of the early Church that were not necessarily hostile to marriage, such as the ideal of martyrdom. Another path lay open to the *matrona*'s spiritual advisers, that of contesting the ascetic claim to the inheritance of the martyrs.

The Martyr Exemplum

From the end of the fourth century on, the legendary heroes of the age of apostles and martyrs functioned both as objects of devotion and as patterns for the spiritual progress of the faithful. We have seen that the faithful might in turn imitate aspects of the martyr's conduct, and that virgins such as Macrina or Eustochium were praised by drawing attention to the relation between their own virtue and that of Thecla of Iconium. Both the *Treatise on Virginity* of Athanasius of Alexandria and the anonymous Greek *Homily on Virginity* preserved among the writings of Basil of Caesarea exhort young women to pattern themselves after Thecla.[42] A late sixth-century homily on penitence addressed to virgins frames even the study of Scripture as imitation of Thecla: "Seek after Paul just as Thecla did, that you may hear what is said to you through him."[43]

Now we begin to see as well an attempt to extend the comparison with Thecla beyond the holy virgins of the Church. Thus the anonymous *Life of Olympias* represents the holy widow (d. 410) as one whose progress in "the path which leads to heaven" was accomplished by "tracing the footsteps" of Thecla.[44] Similarly, the ending restored by Michel Aubineau to an anonymous homily on Thecla (*BHG* 1720) draws a moral from Thecla's fortitude to be shared equally by widows, married women, prostitutes, and virgins: "That each, living in the purity (*katharotēta*) appropriate to her estate, effect in her soul the contemplation of Christ the Lord."[45]

Augustine's *On Holy Virginity*, however, seems to imply that virgins felt that they had a special claim to imitation of Thecla on account of their own virginity. He proposes as a model for married women Crispina of Theveste, one of Africa's great married martyrs, and warns that a virgin should not scorn her married sister, "For how does she know whether while she herself may not yet be able to be a Thecla, the other may already be a Crispina?"[46]

The fifth-century *Life of Syncletica* goes even further, by proposing that the ascetic who imitates Thecla outstrips not only the married, but even in some sense the saint herself:

For if the one Savior was the object of their desires, there necessarily was one opponent for them. And I understand the gentler sufferings to be Thecla's, for the evil of the enemy attacked her from the outside. But with Syncletica he displays his more piercing evil, moving from the inside by means of opposing and destructive thoughts.[47]

At the same time, we see an increasing claim for virginity of the praise traditionally accorded to marriage. Thus Jerome's *Against Jovinian* implies that it is not married women but the virgins of the Church who best emulate the virtuous *matronae* of ancient Rome.[48] In the pseudo-Leucian *Acts of Matthew*, when the apostle defends the virgin Ephigenia from a marriage proposal by the king Hyrtacus, he does so in terms that propose the girl as betrothed already to a more powerful king.[49] Although marriage itself is not denigrated, the implication is that its customary honor should be transferred to those who refuse to marry here on earth.

For *matronae*, the success of the ascetic movement meant a disruption of inherited patterns for negotiating status. The introduction of a new set of criteria for evaluating claims to moral superiority was especially important for women, whose standing had always depended on the projection of moral excellence, all the more since their opportunities to perform deeds of valor or other status-enhancing acts were limited. In addition, women of rank would have been particularly alive to these issues of status because they were expected to set an example for their social inferiors.

As they sought to describe and interpret their own experience, the women of late antiquity may not have seen themselves as women in gendered terms; we, for whom "woman" is an important interpretive category, tend to derive what may be a false generality for a society to which class and estate were the dominant signifiers, and which expected its members to identify at once with multiple relational roles. Christian *matronae*, for example, would have perceived themselves not in solidarity with, but in opposition to married women of lower status in some cases and against aristocratic virgins or pagan *matronae* in others.

We must strain here to capture the vivid late Roman sensitivity to one's status not as subject but as object—that is, as object of scrutiny. Late Romans of both sexes were fiercely concerned with reputation and gifted with a fine instinct for the parameters of verisimilitude. What might be called the late Roman sense of identity depended less on what you knew yourself to be than on what you feared or hoped others might believe.

Christian *matronae* were equally concerned with reputation, or with what they would have called *fama* and what we in our jargon would call "the negotiation of status." Our sources trade regularly in the parody of what they dismiss as *garrula conversatio*[50]—a term we might almost translate as "female competitiveness"—but we should not forget that, in the *ecclesia* no less than in the *saeculum,* the issues at stake in the naming and interpretation of identity and experience were felt to be urgent. An enabling narrative of self-understanding, by which private experience could be given shape and consequence, was central to the work of projecting a public face.

Even the noble and wealthy among married women could but envy the prestige that sexual renunciation conferred in the race for social and spiritual prowess. It was not uncommon, for example, for a married woman to let it be known publicly, with a view to garnering spiritual renown, that she was withholding conjugal rights from her husband.[51] And not all virgins were immune to the competitive spirit of the society from which they had vowed to retire. Since the Jovinianist controversy of the 390s, more than one Christian writer had come to be troubled by the self-congratulation of certain factions within the ascetic movement. Men like Augustine and Pelagius had (each in his own way) addressed an incipient pastoral crisis: would an undue stress on the virginal ideal deprive married Christians of due consolation and encouragement?[52]

In part, this tension was resolved by the creation of a two-tiered system within the Church, with the stars of the ascetic movement emulating the ascetic heroes and heroines of yore, while the remainder of men and women—those who maintained the rituals and duties of the Greco-Roman household—were left with the less desirable role of praising another's zeal.

But where women were concerned, another factor was at work. Whereas the battle over the romantic heroine recorded in the Apocryphal Acts was waged for rhetorical purposes—to vivify the opposition between Christian otherworldliness and the networks of reproduction, kinship, and alliance of the *saeculum*—we have little evidence that the authors of the Apocryphal Acts considered the effect their heroines might have on the self-understanding and behavior of actual women. Instead, the romantic heroine was supposed to carry a rhetorical message about men. In the fifth and sixth centuries, by contrast, the widespread adaption of Christian literary forms to the uses of the leisured and literate classes resulted in a new, perhaps unprecedented, attention to the problem of how female readers might apprehend the Christian heroines and how the heroines themselves might be adapted to devotional use.

Most at issue was how women would interpret the connection between Christian perfection, as expressed in martyrdom, and the sexual abstinence that had come to be associated with it.[53] Although the ascetic movement had initially served to supplement Christianity's narrow spectrum of sacred roles and priesthoods, it resulted in a further diminution of religious identity for the women and men who could claim neither clerical status nor ascetic stature. For married women the problem was particularly acute, since women's symbolic position as representatives of the household left them especially vulnerable to the erosion of the *domus* as the central icon of the social imagination.

The pastoral problem of addressing the *matrona* who felt herself excluded by the rising prestige of asceticism appears repeatedly and in unexpected places across the devotional literature of the fifth and sixth centuries. We turn now to the hagiographical "novels" of fifth- and sixth-century Rome. These inventive rereadings of Christian romance constitute our best evidence for the reaction of readers to the romantic heroine of the Apocryphal Acts. We can see from yet another series of narrative subversions that Christian writers took seriously the problem of how real-life women might be affected by the peculiarities of a literary heroine. We will also see that, as civic religion lost ground, the ascetic Christianity replacing it had to contend with new stresses.

· 6 ·

The Imprisoned Heroine

A final series of texts, the *Gesta* (Deeds) of the Roman martyrs, offers us a glimpse of the imaginary world of *matronae* as they sought to understand the change to their status wrought by Christianization. Little known but preserved in extravagant quantities, the *Gesta* are pious fictions written in Rome during the fifth and sixth centuries to honor the martyrs of that city. They can be distinguished from the genuine pre-Constantinian Acts of the Martyrs by their novelistic format. In particular, they refract the heroine of romance through yet another lens, that of the Roman Church as it settled into the comfortable habits of medieval piety. For the most part, the *Gesta* adopt the now-established outline of the heroine as the ascetic embodiment of Christian purity and spiritual power. But if read carefully, certain of the *Gesta* reveal an unease with the heroine's transformation. The troubling question seems to have been this: in her new guise as a devotional model, would the ascetic heroine encourage or discourage the piety of the *matronae* on whom the Church had come to depend?

Nearly a century ago, Albert Dufourcq proposed that the *Gesta* were written to promote the Roman cult of martyrs, which in turn was the main element of a Catholic effort to combat the popularity of Manichaeism. The Manicheans, it will be remembered, were the champions of strict asceticism, and from the time of Jovinian Catholic writers had to acknowledge the good of marriage or face a charge of heresy. By the reign of Leo the Great in the mid fifth century, Dufourcq argued, the tide had turned and the Catholics were in close competition with the Manicheans over which group could lay claim to the ascetic ideal.[1] Because the *Gesta* have received no systematic study since Dufourcq's day, it is difficult to evaluate his hypothesis. But the *Gesta* often conflate martyrdom and virginity,[2] and it is entirely possible that the texts were designed to support the Catholic assertion of the value of the human body against Manichaean dualism by chronicling the heroic suffering of the martyrs, while at the same time averting a Manichaean monopoly on ascetic virtue.

In creating these heroes and heroines, the *Gesta* wove together narrative strands from the ancient romances and the Apocrpyphal Acts of the Apostles around historical personages who were partly or entirely imaginary. This process of literary conflation and reuse had the effect of obscuring any distinction between the spiritual trials of the pre-Constantinian martyrs and those of the aristocratic virgins of fifth-century Rome. Thus the *Gesta* lent literary weight to the ascetic vocation by assimilating it to an earlier tradition of literature and to the increasingly powerful martyr cult.[3]

Devotion to an exemplary figure implied, but did not require, a point of identification between the object of devotion and the devotee. In theory, such identification was unnecessary. The exemplum was there for all to contemplate, and each could and should bring away what was most useful to his or her estate.[4] The struggle of heroes and heroines to preserve their bodily and spiritual purity was meant to afford morally elevating contemplation to an audience less than exemplary, who would hear the martyrdom accounts read aloud in the liturgy of the appropriate feast day.[5]

Yet while the revision of martyrs as ascetic heroines made for compelling narrative, it caused tensions within the Church because of its seeming exclusion of the married laity. In practice, men and women tended to stress any possible point of identification between themselves and the object of their devotion. Jerome, refusing to acknowledge the married clergy, had put the question: "[Does] he abide in Christ or not? If he abide, let him walk as Christ walked. But if there is rashness in professing to copy the virtues of our Lord, he does not abide in Christ, for he does not walk as did Christ."[6] Too strong an emphasis on the virginal ideal could have unintended results. What most Roman women had in common was their certain exclusion from any claim to the crown of martyrdom, if that claim required a vow of perpetual virginity. For a heroine to serve these women as an invitation to the seemingly endless struggle of the *imitatio Christi*, she must inspire admiration and affection, but she must do so without seeming entirely forbidding in her perfection, lest her exemplary qualities discourage any attempt at imitation.

The place of ascetic virtue—of virginity or abhorrence for conjugal relations—in the construction of the *Gesta*'s heroines has not received the attention it deserves, partly because of a confusion over literary genre. Although the *Gesta martyrum* mimic the content of the pre-Constantinian *Acta martyrum*, in form and intention they are closer to the Christian romance genre exemplified by the Apocryphal Acts of the Apostles. The fatal democracy of the Acts of the Martyrs, with their commemoration of the courage of real historical individuals without regard to social class or marital status, was not entirely satisfying to a community whose members showed boundless interest in rank and status, whether in spiritual or social terms. This meant that in devising a heroine the *Gesta* followed the ancient romances and the Apocryphal Acts in preferring a figure who would elicit admiration for her wealth, family, and beauty, even as she shone in matters of bodily and spiritual purity. Such attributes would reinforce the heroine's personal magnetism and spiritual power: an audience was expected to sympathize most deeply with the heroine in whom least fault could be found.

But the Manichaeans argued that to venerate the martyrs was no better than idolatry. As early as 397 or 398, Augustine had defended the martyr cult against a Manichaean opponent by arguing that moral betterment of the faithful, not worship, was the real purpose of such piety.[7] This meant that Christian writers had to present the martyr's struggle as one that all Christians would endure as they attempted to resist the temptation to vice. This reading countered the imputation of idolatry, but it resulted in yet another pastoral problem, for it made it all the more possible for those whose personal characteristics coincided with those of the exemplum to claim that it was they and not others who were closest to perfect imitation.

The confusion caused by this rift between theory and practice was aggravated by the tension between Catholicism and Manichaeism. That the heroines of the Apocryphal Acts were perceived as rejecting domestic virtues—despite the representation of continence as a sort of hyper-chastity—may be one reason why the literature built around them was plagued by suspicions of heresy throughout antiquity. We know from references in the Manichaean Psalm Book that the Manichaeans laid claim to the heroines of the Apocryphal Acts as their own.[8] This meant that both the orthodox and their opponents drew on the heroines, and yet each might accuse the other of a wrong interpretation. Thus Augustine's contemporary, Evodius of Uzala, characterized Maximilla's evasion of Aegeates in the *Acts of Andrew* as a dangerous Manichaean business[9] even as Augustine was defending the veneration of the martyrs against a Manichaean charge of idolatry. We will see in one of the *Gesta*, the little-known *Passio Anastasiae*, an attempt to "stabilize" an ascetic heroine—that is, to suggest that for women to venerate and even imitate her did not mean that the devotees themselves had to reject the married estate.

Christian Mediocrity

The *Passio* recorded for Saint Anastasia preserves what seem to be traces of a fifth-century discussion of how Christian devotional exempla should be constituted, and whether the virginal ideal could serve to guide the spiritual progress of women who were (or had been) married. The *Passio* cannot be said to offer the most explicit surviving discussion of the tensions that the virginal ideal might cause for married women— the palm for that must go to the *Liber ad Gregoriam*. Still, some attention to the *Passio* is in order, since it is in the *Gesta martyrum* that we possess the actual proposal of ascetic exempla to a population that could hardly hope to emulate them.

That the martyr Anastasia was seen as a particularly appropriate exemplum for married women is clear from the *Liber ad Gregoriam*. The connections between the *Passio* and the *Liber* are specific enough that it seems clear that one author was familiar with the other, although the direction of the influence is not immediately obvious.[10] The conjunction between the two texts offers a possibility rare in the study of female piety in late antiquity. Through the preservation of two voices addressing the problem of how women might respond to the same devotional exemplum in two related but different literary genres, we may move one step closer to asking how women's devotional lives were affected by these exempla.

One episode in particular of the *Passio*, an exchange of letters between Anastasia and her spiritual adviser Chrysogonus, seems designed to address an aspect of the spiritual life that would have been particularly relevant to married women. If the characteristics of an exemplum differed too patently from the aspirations of those it was meant to encourage, the force of its example could be inverted, becoming an instrument of exclusion where rivals for good repute stood ready to call attention to one another's shortcomings in the pursuit of sanctity. For married women, whose state of life lacked the preferred lineaments of feminine sanctity, a protective self-interpretation would become the paramount method of perseverance in virtue.

The *Liber ad Gregoriam* addresses Anastasia precisely as a martyr whose own trials in marriage might serve to encourage her married sisters. To enhance this point of identification, the *Liber* blurs the distinction between Anastasia's martyrdom and her earthly marriage:

> How many wives sprung from a lowly condition must have scoffed at physical threats, and in the face of a raging tyrant—not pale with fear, but eager in the Lord—when they saw that you (who are noble and dainty) constantly scorned all kinds of torments, for the defense of honor and faith? (5)

The *Liber*'s initial praise of Anastasia leaves unclear whether her encounter with a tyrant refers to her public martyrdom or to her trials during marriage, a move that makes it possible to compare the experience of other married women directly to Anastasia's own. In the *Passio* the torments Anastasia endures from her husband are understood explicitly as a preparation for public martyrdom. The *Liber* continues, however, by turning to her public martyrdom, expounding its theological significance as the confirmation of the sanctity of a woman whose second-class status among the married might otherwise seem to exclude her as a candidate for Christian heroism. On the contrary, the *Liber* reasons, Anastasia's participation in the compromised married state confers on her an exceptional claim to importance as one who made the Christian message available to a wider audience. The *Liber*'s author saw this claim reflected in the fact that Saint Anastasia's feast day fell on the 25th of December, a certain sign that her martyrdom was destined for a most important role in Christ's work of redemption:

Justly Christ took you up into the heavens on the same day on which he himself descended to Earth, and he permitted the anniversary of your martyrdom to occur on the same day as the nativity of his assumption [of the flesh], because you, by suffering martyrdom, offered to many what He offered to all by being born. And just as, having despised majesty, he took on the form of a servant, so that he might assist us all, so you yourself, having despised the glory of nobility, took on an ignominy of person, so that you might be imitated by others, and so that you might provide a model of Christian endurance for all. You will receive everlasting glory as much because you set an example for the edification of all matrons (*pro aedificatione omnium matronarum*) as because of your own martyrdom. (5)

The *Liber*'s exultant sense of Anastasia's singular merit as a married Christian heroine may seem disproportionate, since she was not the only married martyr venerated at Rome; nor was hers the only *Passio* preserved from the group.[11] Until recently, though, little attention has been paid to the fact that Anastasia's legend acknowledges her as a married woman. She is widowed early in the story, and scholarly tradition has tended to remember her as a widow rather than as a *matrona*. Presumably this served to dissociate the saint from the stain of conjugal relations: indeed, Lenain de Tillemont in the seventeenth century handed down the claim that throughout her marriage Anastasia was able to preserve her virginity.[12]

The *Passio* itself dwells in some detail on Anastasia's misadventures as a married woman, and we will do the same with a view to understanding how these trials were meant to serve the spiritual progress of the *Passio*'s audience. As the story opens, Anastasia is in a particularly delicate situation. She is married to a pagan husband, Publius, who not only refuses to see the merit of her steadfast ministry to Christian prisoners but who responds to her activity with revulsion. A clue to Publius' outrage may lie in Anastasia's exchange of her matronal regalia for mean attire during her forays into the street. When this is brought to his attention, Publius gives the order that Anastasia be imprisoned at home. We know from Augustine's letter to Edicia that for a married woman of standing to adopt humble garb during public appearances might be understood as an advertisement that sexual relations between the couple had ceased.[13] This may have been understood as the implication of Anastasia's gesture—which, if contrary to the wishes of Publius, would have represented a substantial insult to his honor.

The detention of Anastasia within her own home carries a number of meanings. In the first place, it points to a comparison between Anastasia and the married heroines of the Apocryphal Acts, at least one of whom faced imprisonment by her husband.[14] Second, it serves a narrative purpose of identifying Anastasia with the imprisoned Christian confessors to whom she has ministered and among whom she will take her place as the story progresses. Finally, Anastasia's imprisonment may be read as an acknowledgment to the *Passio*'s audience of the plight of any married woman, whose position and responsibilities within the household might bar her from certain aspects of Christian practice—including the vow of virginity—to which she might otherwise commit herself.

It would be injudicious to concur with Lenain de Tillemont in deducing from Anastasia's love of chastity that her marriage has not involved sexual relations, for the text explicitly states that her troubles with her husband begin "at the time when she left off relations with her husband *(mariti consortio)*, on the pretext of a feigned illness."[15] (There is little doubt as to the sexual meaning of *mariti consortium* here.) This supports the inference above that it is the disruption of conjugal relations—or the affront to honor that publication of the fact implies—which causes the wrath of Publius. The brief characterization of the rift between Anastasia and Publius recapitulates the scenario drawn from the Apocryphal Acts in which a pagan husband and a Christian wife are set at odds by her sudden refusal of the marriage bed after months or years of what must have been consensual relations.

In the Apocryphal Acts, the disruption of conjugal relations typically followed the formation of a spiritualized lovers' triangle: the wife would refuse her husband his conjugal rights once she heard the preaching of the apostle. In the case of Anastasia, however, the sequence is somewhat altered. On the one hand, at the story's beginning Anastasia has already professed Christianity. On the other, the animosity that arises between Anastasia and Publius is cut short not by the martyrdom of Chrysogonus—or by her own—but by the death of the husband himself.

It is only after the death of Publius that Anastasia's real adventures take place, according to her *Passio*. Yet the early scenes are important for understanding the constitution of Anastasia as a model for other women. Although the *Passio* does not set the device of a married woman's friendship with a male mentor to its customary purpose with regard to the hero's martyrdom, the *Passio* does make use of an antagonism between husband and spiritual mentor as a narrative force. Anastasia's painful circumstances at the mercy of an evil husband are offered to explain her boldness in soliciting the aid of Chrysogonus at the outset. It is during the worst of the trials inflicted by her husband that Anastasia requests the holy man's guidance.

The initial exchange of letters between Anastasia and Chrysogonus plays a complex role in the *Passio,* mediating between the sufferings of the married Anastasia and her subsequent widowhood and martyrdom. The correspondence is primarily an exegesis of the proto-martyrdom to which Anastasia, soon to take on the mantle of martyrdom itself, is being subjected. We know, again from the *Liber ad Gregoriam,* that a woman's lack of fortitude in the trials of marriage could be used to question whether her yearning for a more public martyrdom was in earnest: "In sum, why are you unwilling to bear the small trials, who are sure you can bear the greater ones?" (5). The *Passio Anastasiae* takes a more humane approach to the same problem. The correspondence between Chrysogonus and Anastasia is intended to make married women understand the importance of the trials they bear, with Anastasia's suffering as the hermeneutical key to their own.

Anastasia's first letter to Chyrsogonus reads as follows:

Anastasia to the holy confessor Chrysogonus. Despite the fact that my father was a worshipper of idols, my mother, Fausta, always lived in a way that was chaste and exceedingly Christian. She baptized me while I was still quite young. However, I had the misfortune of being married off to a sacrilegious man, from whose bed, by the Grace of God, I have been able to escape, and instead I embrace day and night the path trodden by our Lord Jesus Christ. (4)

The woman goes on to explain her circumstances: her husband has put her under surveillance day and night, "like a magician or a profaner of the sacred *(veluti magam atque sacrilegam)*." The conditions of her imprisonment are so grave that she fears for her life. She declares her intent to follow in the footsteps of the saints, if she should survive to do so. If her present trials end in death, she entreats Chrysogonus to protect against a reversal by her husband of her benefactions to the Church, even as she rejoices in a martyr's death.

Here, in Anastasia's own assertion, we find an important clue to the *Passio*'s revision of the martyr exemplum. The *Passio* addresses two aspects of spiritual challenge specific to the experience of married women. The first is the sense of helplessness in the face of a husband's decision to obstruct her disposition of time and resources. While comparatively much is known of the autonomy that some women enjoyed by law, we know little about a woman's ability to realize legal rights. Anastasia's exhortation to Chrysogonus invokes the aid of the Christian community, with the aid of God, against her husband's defiance of her right to give her own property to the Church.

The second aspect, which would have been common to any Christian witness enacted in isolation, was the difficulty of sustaining Christian meaning where no community existed to receive and validate the messages carried by Christian speech and gesture. Though public forms of Christian witness—however exacting they might be—offered the prospect of an equally public affirmation by the faithful, the witness of Christians acting in isolation ran the risk of senselessness and despair. Anastasia closes her epistle with the words, "Vale, vir dei, et memento mei." While an exhortation to prayer on the writer's behalf is common in the Christian epistolary tradition, the choice of wording—*memento mei* means both "pray for me" and "remember me"—evokes the importance of recognition and the promise of remembrance as sources of strength for Christian heroism.

Ideally, the labors of the heroic Christian woman would be validated by the response of her community; in turn, the community would be strengthened by seeing those same labors performed. But this process of confirmation could do little for those whose witness went without benefit of a sympathetic audience. The reality was that the heroism of daily life was as likely to go unrecorded in the fifth century as in any other period of history; what the *Passio* could do, however, was to resolve this failing within the sanctuary of narrative. If married women could not be assured that their trials within the *domus* would be perceived and encouraged by the watchful eye of the Christian community, they could at least be reassured that the community worshipped a God who *would* perceive and encourage hidden martyrs and that the community was prepared symbolically to honor the trials of a married woman as a fitting substitute for public martyrdom.

Thus Anastasia's cultivation of a spiritual mentor in the early scenes of the *Passio* should be read not only literally, as the heroine's request for spiritual guidance, but also in terms of its narrative function of assuring readers that Anastasia's first preparation for martyrdom, her testing through the instrument of a difficult husband, had received the recognition and encouragement of the Christian community in the person of Chrysogonus. If the *Passio* was indeed read forth in a liturgical setting, this recognition would have been multiplied in the narrative present, as Anastasia's deeds were renewed in the memory of the community; the encouragement would have been multiplied in the hearts of those who felt that their own unacknowledged situation reflected Anastasia's early trials.

Chrysogonus' response to Anastasia's letter develops this theme, although it may seem at first to be less than sensitive to her plight. Without prefatory compassion, he exhorts his noble correspondent to the virtue of endurance. He continues by admonishing her to avoid all temptation to sin (advice that might seem heavy-handed, considering her circumstances). But if we read Chrysogonus' response with an eye to the *Passio*'s economy of memory and recognition, we may discern the solidarity with Anastasia's suffering that the *Passio*'s audience would have heard in these words.

Read as a gesture of protection against the insidious dangers of despair, the letter's abruptness is revealed as urgency born from compassion. Chrysogonus admonishes: "Take care that you not be deceived by trials in the midst of an otherwise holy life. It is not that God has tricked you; rather, God is testing your faith" (5). When Chrysogonus exhorts Anastasia to avoid sin, what he means to warn against is the disempowering sin of doubt, for her courage will hinge on her ability to keep the faith, and to imagine a final significance for the trials she encounters. If she weakens in her conviction that her suffering is a divine test—that her suffering is meaningful—she risks losing the momentum she has gathered through the force of her own self-understanding. Once she has lost the interpretive thread afforded by the spirituality of martyrdom, she may herself become lost in the senselessness of an experience that was itself, while it was invested with significance, the best possible preparation for martyrdom. In this way Chrysogonus' letter to Anastasia amplifies one of the central pastoral strands of the *Passio Anastasiae* itself: the offer of a remedy to the aporia of a soul facing trials to which no sense or meaning has been assigned.

The problem of senselessness is but one version of the predicament of the woman whose exercise of spiritual gifts is constrained by feminine propriety. The predicament is a recurring theme in the literature of female sanctity: we know from subsequent periods, for which we possess first-person accounts by women, that the constraints of propriety, particularly if seemingly arbitrary, were felt to be spiritually disabling even as they were infuriating.[16] Although the spiritual meaning of adversity and suffering is a recurring patristic theme, a psychological emphasis on the danger of misinterpreting one's own experience—and thus of succumbing to discouragement or despair—must have had a particular importance in devotional literature for women.[17]

It is in this light that the *Passio Anastasiae*'s emphasis on interpretation should be read. Where obstacles barred a woman from altering the broad outline of her circumstances or actions, a greater importance was correspondingly placed in strategies of interpretation through which available experience and agency could be mined for significance and affirmation. The need for compensatory strategies of self-interpretation must have been felt especially keenly by married women, whose status and duties afforded far less opportunity to accommodate a chosen religious identity than did those of the consecrated virgin.

Because virgins were in a position of autonomy compared to their married peers, the praise of female virginity might be salt in the wounds of the married. No matter how sublime the Christian piety of a married woman, she would lose heart if she believed that by definition she could only be a second-class citizen in the city of God. Where it was understood as defining an exclusive membership of the elect, the praise of virginity hardened into a glass ceiling. Instead of offering an invitation to virtue, the equation of martyrdom with virginity ran the risk of denying a Christian identity precisely to those most in need of the power of Christian discourse to maintain a tenuous but all-important view of the self.

Concern for this kind of pastoral backfiring motivated the writing of the *Liber ad Gregoriam*, and it is not impossible that a similar anxiety motivated the writing—or the redaction—of the *Passio Anastasiae* as well. Still, while so much remains to be discovered of the occasions and motives for the production and redaction of the various *Gesta martyrum*, it is too early to stress any one motive over others. The tension between marriage and virginity as Christian vocations may have owed as much to the competition between religious groups as to the competition between individuals. When we return to the *Passio Anastasiae* we will see how its interest in marriage was fed by the conflict between Christian orthodoxy and Manichaeism.

Self-Understanding and Spiritual Rivalry

The *Liber ad Gregoriam* takes up the problem of the discouraged *matrona* in the language of conflict within the Christian soul between the vices and the virtues. The goal remains the reinforcement of a Christian's ability to interpret her or his own achievement in the face of the perhaps more spectacular successes achieved by others. For the *Liber*, this emphasis on correct self-understanding is seen as all the more relevant to the married, who might be unseated by the more emphatic claims to virtue of their peers in the ascetic life.

Augustine had foreseen the possibility of such wrangling between ascetics and the married, but the *Liber*'s treatment of identity is adapted from the literature of the ascetic communities themselves. Indeed, the ascetic community was a laboratory for the study of the vulnerability of Christians before their peers and the fragility of an individual's claim to Christian identity. John Cassian's fifth-century *Conferences*, for example, reads like a dissertation on the mental instability of the ascetic.[18] Book 14 treats at length the problem of the monk whose dedication to his own humble pursuit of perfection is undermined by the example of another whose vocation is more visibly glorious, a problem common to those not yet well established in their profession. Cassian exhorts the unsettled monk not to leave his own path in order to imitate someone who seems to be following one more arduous. If he pursues the virtues indiscriminately—according to an impulse of the moment, however noble—he will achieve perfection in none of them: the result will only be a lack of monastic *stabilitas,* a hindering of spiritual development. Indeed, "God is reached by many paths, and each must pursue the path he has chosen with constancy, so that he reach perfection by it, whatever it be." The ascetic who leads others to doubt their own vocation is revealed as one whose claim to purity is false:

> Take care not to follow the example of those, who have acquired the habit of holding forth . . . and because they know how to speak elegantly and with abundance on whatever subject pleases them, pass for having spiritual science to the eyes of those who have not learned how to assess their true character. But it is one thing to have a facility in speaking . . . and another to enter into the heart and the marrow of celestial sayings and to contemplate deep and hidden mysteries with the purest eye of the heart.[19]

Here we are well away from the debate on marriage and well into the very core of monastic language and monastic thinking, with their characteristic distrust of worldly success and skill, where these were turned against the well-being of the community or against the fragile courage of its members. The communities under discussion are not of course identical, but the continuity of approach bespeaks the fact that monastic and lay literature were often produced by the same writers, grounded in the same religious sensibility.

We can see in the *Liber ad Gregoriam* a curious use of literary genre to shape the reader's perception of social reality. The *Liber* sets an allegorical dialogue, in which the vices and virtues contest one another's claim on the reader's soul, into a frame narrative where a dialogue is already underway between the narrator, addressing the reader in the second person, and the reader, who may object to the author's message. The use of reported direct speech in the frame falls squarely within the recommended techniques of lively oratory as defined by Quintillian and others. Yet this direct speech combines with the formal *altercatio* between vices and virtues in a particularly dense blend. Its purpose: to dramatize the spiritual danger to Christians posed by competition, particularly competition over the claim to Christian identity.

The *Liber* itself is generally cast in the second person, as advice to the individual reader, while the allegorical dialogue shifts from second to third and first persons, as the narrator turns to describe the spiritual combat and then to report what is being said by the opponents. The reported speech shifts between first and second persons as the interlocutors shift their attention between self and opponent—that is, between defensive and aggressive rhetoric.

To complicate the matter further, the second-person address to the reader ("Dear girl, do not fear a fleeting sadness") is frequently interrupted by reported expostulations from various imaginary speakers ("You will hear that with one voice they respond to your question thus")—again, as in the allegorical dialogue, shifting between first and second persons. Second-person interventions frequently illustrate how an unsympathetic acquaintance might interpret the addressee's struggle to cultivate Christian virtue, followed by the author's advice on how to put such a critic in her place.

The first-person speeches tend to fall into three categories: they are self-justificatory (like the suggested replies to the unsympathetic interlocutor), or they offer friendly advice to the reader—hints from the spiritually successful—or they record the remorse and repentance of those who have already fallen into error. In each case, the first-person narratives offer evaluations (positive or negative) of an individual's spiritual achievement. These expostulations echo and reinforce the serpentine expressions of the vices in the allegorical dialogue; in the end, the setting of the dialogue in this context of self-justificatory declamations serves to imply that the reader's unfriendly peers should be understood as spokeswomen for the vices themselves.

This polyphony reflects a context identifiable as that of the Roman *matrona*. While each individual is held accountable for her own spiritual success or failure, and indeed to some extent for that of those around her, there is a degree to which meaning is negotiable. The voices of the *Liber* engage in a seemingly endless liturgy of interpretation, whether justifying their own behavior, distancing themselves from it (as in the case of repentant sinners), or attempting to evaluate one another's behavior, often with a view to casting the other's actions in an unfavorable light.

Such a variety of competing interpretations could be bewildering. The *matrona*'s rivals might have a vested interest in leading her to misjudge her own achievement—and perhaps to undermine it. Thus a correct understanding of one's own spiritual status was as necessary to spiritual progress for the *matrona* as it was for the monk.

As we turn to the text of the *Liber ad Gregoriam*, we will see that the author leads the reader to appreciate the dangers of spiritual disorientation by constructing the manual itself as a kaleidoscope of conflicting points of view. The *Liber*'s opening section lays out the spiritual peril of the Christian who is uncertain of her vocation and may fall prey to discouragement: "And so, I do not want you to think that sadness can destroy you, if you receive it as one well-established in charity; yet through whomsoever it may have come upon you, it is inflicted by the Devil." It is interactions with others who undermine her sense of Christian purpose that are seen as the prime threat. The *Liber* frames other Christian women not as fellow travelers or well-intentioned comrades, but as worldly and malicious rivals who seek to cast a negative interpretation on the reader's Christian works. For the *Liber*'s author, Christian identity is a matter of the establishment of a mutual discourse, a give-and-take of narrative in which one Christian evaluates the religious identity proposed by the other.

This is perhaps most visible in the allegorical dialogue, where spiritual malaise figures as a peril in the domain of human speech. Even the temptation to commit actual, concrete sins is assimilated to the rubric of sins of mis-speech. Temptation appears in allegorical guise as an aristocratic woman, daughter of the Devil, who competes with the reader in a legal battle in the heavenly courts. When she faces Temptation, the addressee is encouraged to remember that if Temptation is the Devil's daughter, she herself is the daughter of God.

> ... defend the nobility of your lineage, and if the daughter of the Devil—that is, without doubt, a delighting in any sin whatsoever, or an opportunity for whatever kind of crime—has attempted to capture you, then protest that you, the daughter of the High King, have been unlawfully dishonored by the daughter of a captive barbarian. Then protest vigorously and unsparingly: use the privilege of your nobility, claim for yourself the prerogative of power to rule; bring in the Apostles as intercessors, introduce the army of white-clad martyrs. (2)

To resist Temptation is to show a daughter's loyalty to the heavenly family.

The marriage relationship can itself become a vehicle for a debilitating rivalry. The Devil stands ready to foster self-interest precisely because of the spiritual power of a married couple's harmony. Far from being a guarantee of spiritual failure, then, marriage is a brave gesture of defiance calling for a heightened vigilance against the Devil's snares.

> For already at the very beginning of marriage ... the author of all crime presaged that you would be his assassin, nor from any other motive did he attempt either at first to incite quarrelling between you, or afterwards to plant the seed of various instances of discord, except that he—the Devil—might separate those joining together against him and wishing to live in the love of Christ. (1)

This idea of marital concord as a Christian achievement is continuous with the position of the Christian traditionalists discussed earlier.

For the female partner in the marriage, there is an additional complication. If the conjugal bond fails and the spouses take their grievance to the heavenly courts, it is to the disadvantage of the wife, who bears responsibility for maintaining concord. Her position as bearer of virtue can function to her advantage:

> Show ... how fastidious you are in the service of charity, how decorous in compliance to a command, so that—bound by consideration of this—[your husband] may cease to keep his own counsel, and will receive your whole will as a divine pattern, and will shiver at your displeasure as at sacrilege. (7)

But if the semblance of conjugal unity is breached, it is the wife who will be held accountable:

> You will be blessed if, standing in front of the tribunal of Christ on that day [of judgement], you are able to say, "Here, Lord, is the man whom you ordained should be my husband: I guided him by so great a compliance of manner that he never held out against my will ..." how ungodly, how very bitter it will be if, God forbid, being bound by the ties of certain sins, he should complain before the Judge, "The woman whom You gave to me, she herself has made a spirit of fury and anger hold sway in me, and made me sin by her continual scorn. It is through her that I have fallen into this crime ... her worthlessness has caused this sin, her haughtiness has caused that one." (8)

Fundamentally, we are still within the boundaries of the moral language of womanly influence and *sōphrosynē*, self-control.

What is different here is the acute mistrust of the claims and accusations by which status and identity are negotiated. The system has broken down, and the abuses a woman will encounter can mislead even the most sincere of Christians, if she has not been adequately trained in interpretation:

> For thus is the name of vice attached to every kind of virtue, so that the faithful one is called idle, the faithless, refined. Through which the vices so take the place of the virtues in human minds, that less-instructed simplicity judges what it sees pleasing mortals as what should be followed. (4)

To be lured into this kind of semantic grappling is a trap. The Christian cannot benefit from being drawn into a competition of naming. She will be taunted by others who may hope to entangle her in the fruitless business of self-justification:

> Why do you open yourself to the reproaches of mortals and to the despising of the mob? . . . why indeed, when you are accused despite your own knowledge of your innocence, do you refrain from speaking, so that you seem to confirm an accusation which you do not refute? (16)

The only safe response is precisely not to respond at all.

But within the world of the narrative, a response must be given, because the moral superiority of the author's position has to be established conclusively. Thus the *Liber* indulges the absurdity of casting the recommended nonresponse in reported dialogue. This is what the reader is encouraged to say to rivals who taunt her falsely:

> The person who is fleeing from a line of swords in hot pursuit has no leisure for tarrying, and pondering over affronts . . . if retribution is to be demanded, it is not in a field where the sword rages that records can be drawn up and the plaintiff call witnesses. In the field of battle, let words fall silent: I will not forsake endurance . . . it is endurance herself who will offer me the safety of the city: let her represent me in the presence of the King. (16)

This is the crux of the problem of Christian identity. The Christian *must* reply to his or her critics, if only to say that the taunts are not worth a reply. The refusal to respond, in turn, is a triumph of sociolinguistic framing: rather than taking up the accusations made by her opponent, the righteous *matrona* accuses her accuser of starting a rivalry whose very terms reveal the accuser's ignorance of the noble ideals of Christian community.

We have seen that the *Liber* encourages its reader to reject the taunts of others while encouraging a certain mean-spirited satisfaction in her own moral superiority. An equal if opposite paradox holds in the injunction to the reader to cultivate disinterested speech *(puritatis index loquella)* (4), speech that is not compromised by rhetorical strategy, even as she is in fact being taught how to defend herself professionally in a context electric with self-promotion.

If we trace the notion of disinterested speech to its roots in classical and Hellenistic moral philosophy, its social function becomes clearer. In our literature, the reader is exhorted to cultivate a pattern of self-presentation that can be dissociated from the constraints and distortions of self-interested positioning, while the same neutral frame is claimed for the interaction between author and reader. If the claim to disinterested speech sets one's own speech against the interested speech of one's peers, to propose disinterested speech to religious followers or a literary patron is both to offer a program of moral elevation for their benefit and to suggest that one's own advice—oral or written—can be relied upon as morally sound.

Here we see the connection to the ancient discourse of *parrhēsia*, frank speech. David Konstan has characterized the shift in meaning of the term from the classical to the Hellenistic period as a shift from the free speech of the classical citizenry to the morally certified frankness or candor of Hellenistic friendship, in polar opposition to the hypocrisy of the self-interested flatterer.[20] This development reflects the replacement of democracy by kingship, and thus new kinds of patronage. The advice of a great man's friends had to be scrutinized for signs of parasitic self-interest, that is, for the tendency to flatter the patron rather than warning him of harsh realities, even though the unpleasant warning might ultimately serve his best interest. The *Nachleben* in late antiquity of this opposition between frank speech and flattery is difficult to trace only because of its ubiquity. It was certainly a commonplace of rhetoric and moral philosophy throughout late antiquity, and would have formed part of the apparatus on which a paraphilosophical work such as the *Liber ad Gregoriam* could draw.

For the most part, the *Liber* approaches disinterested speech from the point of view of the speaker: it exhorts the addressee to conceive of herself as a cultivator of disinterested speech, and therefore as a witness of truth against the false rhetoric of the spiritually misguided. But implicit in this exhortation is an approach to disinterested speech from the point of view of the listener, that is, from the position of one who must distinguish between worthy and unworthy pretenders. The *Liber* frames its addressee as a socially prominent figure who will be surrounded by those whose attempt to cultivate complicity is marred by self-interest, explicitly warning against such pretenders to false intimacy: "Let no one seduce you with empty words: but this is what you may tolerably hear, which is veiled by no cloud of fawning or of flowery speech" (17). If speech can function to claim a false complicity between speaker and listener, the speaker to be trusted is the one who does not shy from unflattering truths. This helps to explain the hectoring tone that characterizes so much epistolary and homiletic advice in late antiquity: a jocular willingness to degrade the audience serves as a sign of the independence—and thus the moral authenticity—of the speaker.

The Merits of Spiritual Teachers

This kind of teasing makes an important point. The persistent if low-grade irony of the *Liber* ("why do you assume you can bear greater trials if you can't bear the lesser ones?") serves not only to underline the perniciousness of the influence of others, but it serves as well to signal the trustworthy nature of the *Liber*'s own influence. Both reader and author knew well that self-interest can function in a variety of ways. Where the *matrona*'s relation to her rivals is concerned, speech functions competitively to frame one's behavior in a positive light and the other's in a light correspondingly negative.

But where the relation between reader and author is in view, the danger of self-interested speech is the creation of a false complicity between speaker and audience. This is the point of the *Liber*'s irony. Precisely the kind of competitive use of speech against which the *Liber*'s author has warned comes into play, not between the addressee and her rivals but between the author and his. A spiritual adviser was by no means unaffected by the cacophony of claims to spiritual prowess: in most cases, the stakes were even higher in the competition among programs (and purveyors) of spiritual instruction.

Fundamentally, the spiritual adviser offered terms by which a believer could be assured that an undeceivable God acknowledged her trials—could achieve, that is, an enabling and encouraging self-interpretation. The spiritual adviser traded on his ability to name the competitive positioning of his listener's other interlocutors. Thus he tried to suggest that while his own advice was disinterested, other claimants to the listener's trust would offer a fawning encouragement as dangerous as secular flattery. Still others—the *matrona*'s peers—were more concerned with asserting their own importance than with a genuine pursuit of virtue. Both flattery and the discouragement of hearing others vaunt their superior spiritual achievements could undermine Christian progress.

The concern to protect aristocratic Christians from the dangerous advice of self-interested advisors may well have served as a coin of mutual accusation among religious specialists. Yet the problem of discerning just whose advice was reliable was universally acknowledged as a serious one. As we saw in the *Conferences* of John Cassian, the derailing of Christians from their set purpose by envy or competition for renown was a major concern of the monastic community. It is not surprising that the interaction among professed ascetics should have been plagued by the same tensions that marked the interaction between ascetics and the laity; this would have seemed especially clear to Cassian, who saw himself as mediating between an asceticism based on the spectacular achievement of single individuals and the cultivation of single-heartedness by a community of individuals.[21] Generations later, Gregory the Great drew together these strands of monastic thinking, developed after Cassian by the Italian cenobitic tradition exemplified in Saint Benedict.[21]

It is perhaps less of a digression than one might imagine to move from discussing Cassian's early fifth-century Conferences to the late sixth-century writings of Gregory: as mentioned above, until it is dated more securely the Liber itself may belong at any point between the two poles.

And of course an important reason for the difficulty of dating the *Liber* is because of the enduring nature of devotional concerns, which often change only imperceptibly from generation to generation.

Gregory's own letters to laywomen reflect his concern for the consolation and encouragement of the "third order" of the Church, the married laity,[23] but they do not indulge in the kind of analysis of self-representation we have seen in the *Liber ad Gregoriam*. Where we do see such a discussion, perhaps not unexpectedly, is in his *Moralia in Job*, which has its origin in sermons preached at Constantinople during the 580s to his monastic companions and other associates.[24] This treatise raises a number of the same points we have seen in the *Liber ad Gregoriam* by taking up the problem of Job, the just *laicus*, for an audience well attuned to the problems of monastic community.[25]

For Gregory, the problem of disruptive claims to particular virtue is often framed as one of assessing the advice proffered by a would-be spiritual mentor. The desire to appear as an authority on the Christian life is often the result of an impulse toward self-promotion, a vice that, like many others, can seem to be the expression of its opposite virtue:

> Certain vices frequently assume the guise of virtues, as, for instance, lavishness wishes to appear like pity, stinginess like frugality, cruelty like justice; in like manner, a desire for empty glory, being unable to keep itself within the bounds of silence, inflames like the zeal of charity, and the powerful desire of ostentation impels a person to speak without restraint, and the desire for display breaks out, as if with the wish of offering advice. (*Moralia in Job*, 23.11.19)

This is a sentiment we have already encountered in chapter 7 of the *Liber*. The polluted discourse of the *saeculum* is all the more pernicious when it is turned to a false claim to holiness.

Gregory is careful to emphasize that it is trials and setbacks, not renown, which are the sign of genuine progress in the Christian life. Those who claim ease of spiritual accomplishment should be unmasked as seekers of glory, men drawn to the spiritual life as an arena for status competition only because of their inability to compete in the more biting climate of the secular arena:

> For there are some persons who, whereas they cannot obtain the glory of the present world by that world's courses of conduct, seek after a

semblance of sanctity, assume the garb of reverence, long to appear imitators of the Old Fathers, and some few things indeed, little and light, they do employ themselves upon, but their strong things, and such as come forth from the root of charity alone, they are indifferent to imitate. (20.14.31)

These seeming experts are in fact agents of the Devil, and their malign influence is not unintentional. Evil is most effective when the allure of good actions is used to bait the victim:

Whence also [the Devil's] members, when they are unable to injure by open wickedness, often assume the guise of a good action . . . for if the wicked were openly evil, they would not be received at all by the good. But they assume something of the appearance of the good, in order that while good men receive in them the appearance which they love, they may take blended with it also the poison which they would avoid. (33.24.44)

This deceptiveness has its limits, however. The visible virtues are unstable when they are not rooted in charity, and thus it is impossible to sustain the farce.

For every dissembler, in that he desires to appear righteous, can never show himself pure in all things, for while he assumes some virtues in hypocrisy, and secretly gives way to vicious habits, some concealed vices speedily break out upon the surface, and exhibit the hide of overlaid hypocrisy.[26]

This is true not only of the false teacher but even of the sincere Christian: "good work is quickly undermined by the tempter if it is ever found unyoked from the bond of charity" (28.22.46). It is only the cultivation of charity, the concern for the well-being of the wider community, which affords real spiritual progress. This will naturally lead to trials and setbacks, but it is the spirit of charity that will provide sustenance in meeting any obstacle.

Gregory emphasizes that serious Christians will take care for the effect their actions have on others. One of the signs of the truly holy is that they

scan their exterior ways round and round that they may furnish good examples in themselves to their brethren, and watchfully mark their interior ways . . . the Psalmist [says] as well of Holy Church that she should be at once beautiful to herself "within" and to others "without," both advancing herself by interior glory, and instructing others by the outward examples of deeds. (19.12.20)

This concern for the effect of one's actions has a venerable patristic background, and we should not be surprised to encounter it again in the *Liber ad Gregoriam*.

While the *Liber* warns its reader to be wary of those who would be her teachers, it also warns her against misusing her own influence on those around her. What is taken for granted is that her actions are oriented to winning the approval of a public, a concern that is turned from a competitive to an edifying purpose. This holds true especially within the province of the family, which is both private and public: private in the sense that it is the most appropriate locus of activity for the modest and chaste *matrona,* and public in the sense that the rules of self-representation are in operation there as in any other community. This tension between public and private is complicated by the fact that the very privacy of the family always served an emblematic, public function.

The most important member of a woman's audience is her husband—an assumption the *Liber* itself occasionally challenges, but more frequently redefines. If she attempts to please him in the worldly terms of sexual attraction, she should attempt equally to do so in the other-worldly terms of spiritual wholesomeness. The two are not seen as necessarily in opposition, but rather as two aspects—one greater and one lesser—of her wifely role.

> This is your real need to please: just as you take care to please nuptial eyes, take care to please the ears, and do not allow any bitterness to come out of your mouth which, having entered marital ears, might declare that you possess an unsightly soul. (7)

This does not mean, however, that the social structure is challenged. Rather, a wife influences her husband toward holiness—obedience to God—through her own obedience. She is imagined at the day of judgment, reminiscing with God on her fine conduct: "just as I complied with him when he was ordering, so he would hearken to you, the gracious Lord ordering him" (8). While the terms are certainly dramatically different, given the balance of power between the sexes, this advice would have been understood to sound the same Pauline theme as Gregory's characterization of the saints, who take care for the effect their behavior will have on the spiritual development of their peers.

Care should be taken to realize that such warnings were not intrinsically misogynistic. Self-consciousness was the hallmark of moral authority for men and women both. Far from undermining the exercise of power, it was a sounding technique. As Conrad Leyser has suggested, one of Gregory's central strategies for confirming his papal authority was "a public rhetoric of vulnerability in power."[27] In the public context, anxiety over one's effect on others was the sign of a man's unwillingness to abuse the good will and admiration of his fellows.

This may serve to contextualize the exhortation in the *Liber ad Gregoriam* that a wife should take exceptional care for the effect her efforts will have on her husband. We see here the fulfillment of Augustine's exhortation that the terms of community in Christian marriage should be no less exacting than those of its monastic counterpart—indeed, when spiritual progress was taken seriously, the obstacles to it were almost precisely the same. Where the *Liber* enjoys ambiguity is in the gendering of this code: the vocabulary of the public man is now applied to the private woman, and yet the woman, after all, must learn not only how best to influence others, but how to do so through the oblique language of the domestic sphere.

Thus the *Liber* adopts the position that there is no need for women's daily lives to be transformed through new roles or new actions, but instead that women should be helped to perceive their usual experience in a spiritually enabling way. We should note, however, that the *Liber* condemns any attempt to move beyond a private discovery of the religious significance of ordinary personal experience into a claim of high standing in the eyes of others. This may be seen as evidence that women did attempt to make just such a connection. But as perceived in the *Liber*, the connection is beside the point. Self-representation, in the sense of justifying one's actions to others, is dismissed as irrelevant—or worse, detrimental—to spiritual progress. We have seen that in both the *Liber* and the *Passio* an attempt was made to accommodate the new stress on self-interpretation by encouraging married women to imagine themselves as the spiritual heirs of the pre-Constantinian martyrs. Finally, though, the *Liber* reassures married women that their limited access to the language of enhanced Christian identity is not a drawback: such self-fashioning will be unnecessary in the only forum where identity matters, the heavenly court of God.

Marriage and Virginity, Manichaeism and Orthodoxy

To conclude, let us return briefly to the hypothesis suggested at the beginning of this chapter, that the *Passio Anastasiae* represents an attempt to "stabilize" an ascetic heroine by making her accessible to the married woman through the technique of reading for identification. Did the emphasis on the spirituality of the *matrona* in the *Liber* and the *Passio* represent a last flicker of the traditionalism of late fourth-century senatorial Christians, or was its context the battle between orthodoxy and Manichaeism of fifth-century Rome? As I have said, any approach to this question will be inconclusive until the material studied by Dufourcq a century ago, the *Gesta martyrum*, is reexamined. But a brief consideration of the Manichaean hypothesis will serve to illustrate the role that *matronae* could still play in the Church long after the rise of the virginal ideal.

Returning for a moment to the relation of the *Passio Anastasiae* and the Apocryphal Acts, we notice that, if the introduction of the husband-wife-apostle triangle lent to the *Passio* the narrative resonance of a familiar romantic heroine, pains had to be taken to avoid identification with the suspect theology of the earlier texts themselves. Indeed, the prologue explicitly defends the *Passio* itself against the charge that to read it out in church, as was the custom on a saint's feast day, is unorthodox:

> I question you who declare these [writings] to be worthy of abolition among the apocryphal writings: by whom is the canon of the Holy Scriptures preserved? Is it not by those who preferred for the sake of that same canon rather to be killed than to be defeated? For what did the martyrs hold to? They held to that faith which is contained in sacred scrolls, in a settled number of books. Taking nothing in preference to the canonical scriptures, we wrote these [writings] out with care, in order to propound the Catholic teaching guarded by the Catholic martyrs. (1)

If their contents were deemed to be of questionable orthodoxy, the *Gesta* would be classed among the apocrypha, the books that might be read for private devotion but not during the liturgy. The *Passio*'s author expresses outrage at the idea of seeing his text dismissed along with precisely the kind of writings it was designed to confront.

We know that, from the late fourth century on, the Apocryphal Acts were believed to have a Manichaean readership. In his treatise *On Heresies* (c. 383) Filastrius of Brescia comments on the circulation of the Apocryphal Acts in Manichaean circles.[28] And in his Letter 64 to Quintianus (c. 401), Augustine warns his fellow presbyter:

> I charge you, then ... not to bring the Church into reproach by reading in the public assemblies those writings which the Canon of the Church has not acknowledged, for by these, heretics, and especially the Manichaeans (of whom I hear some are lurking, not without encouragement, in your district), are accustomed to subvert the minds of the inexperienced. (3)

To subvert the Manichaean practice by substitution did carry the risk of a similar condemnation, but it might gain in effectiveness for drawing on the Manichaean modus operandi.

If the *Passio Anastasiae* was designed to supplement the suspect Apocryphal Acts by an orthodox version of Christian romance, its nod to the spirituality of the married state would have had a significance beyond its explicit pastoral intent. In fact, the initial exchange between Anastasia and Chrysogonus may have been designed precisely to transform the theological implications of the husband-wife-apostle triangle. Although the triangle known from the Apocryphal Acts was often touched by sensationalist overtones, with the wife's repudiation of the husband cast in terms evocative of adulterous passion, the initial exchange of letters between Anastasia and Chrysogonus are characterized by grave formality. Instead of an eroticized encounter between unknowns, the correspondence cultivates a regal distance between the married woman and her spiritual mentor while emphasizing her modest dignity. Thus the *pudor* of the honorable wife Anastasia both criticizes and replaces the frenzied craving for continence of the heroines of the Apocryphal Acts.

Seen in these terms, the acceptance of the *mediocritas* of the married in the *Liber ad Gregoriam* or the *Passio Anastasiae* may itself seem more self-interested. These texts will not accommodate a yearning to understand the historical experience of those at the social margins. They speak quite precisely for the experience of the *pars melior generis humani*—"the better part of the human race"—as understood by the writers, perhaps themselves not so exalted, who served as chaplains to the elite. If they provide for the encouragement of married women, the context of this gesture was a restoration to the senatorial *matrona* in religious terms of the prestige she would claim in a civic context by right of birth. Given the Manichaean stress on virginity, to offer a counter-exemplum designed to recover the allegiance of Christians excluded by the virginal ideal represented an economical strike at Manichaeism's most vulnerable point, especially if these Christians included the socially and economically powerful. This last point may gain in significance as more is understood of the powers exerted by the *matronae* of fifth- and sixth-century Rome through their activity as patrons in secular and ecclesial contexts.[29]

Finally, we should not forget, as we work to understand the religious experience of late Roman and early medieval women, that we know very little about how their self-understanding—or even their interactions with one another and with men—were inflected by issues of wealth and social prestige. A single devotional text offered various and even contradictory messages to its hearers, depending on the experience and circumstances they themselves brought to bear as they read. Where exhortation to virtues such as steadfastness and endurance in adversity were concerned, such interpretive factors had to be especially important. The reception of devotional texts was complicated by conflicting experiences of identity and status even for a single individual: the same *matrona* might inspire respect and even awe among her social inferiors—including the clergy—while retaining an awareness of inferior status among her own peers. How she heard words of consolation or admonition would differ substantially, depending on the speaker.

To stress the difficulty of approaching these aspects of women's religious experience is not to suggest that the task does not merit close attention. On the contrary, precisely because of the need for real progress in our understanding of these important texts and the issues they illuminate, the intent here is to ensure that the investigation does not founder in too much reliance on short-term solutions. We should, I hope, be warned against an easy acceptance of the early Christian literature of continence and rejection of family as a literature of women's autonomy. To such an equation, the question must be put: which women? A second, more far-reaching question follows: what could autonomy itself have meant to a population so deeply committed to the values of group and dynasty? These hard questions both deserve and demand further study.

· Epilogue ·

Looking back across the distance we have traveled, the very landscape of ancient society, based in the relationships and allegiances of the city, has altered in its proportions, along with kinship, dynasty, and the marriage bond as an emblem of social concord. Yet each of these, finally, is still in view. Kinship and dynasty remain central in the middle ages, as central to the great monastic houses as to secular rulers. The symbolic function of the marriage partnership, with the chaste woman persuading her husband to virtue, is alive across the medieval Mediterranean and beyond, from the tenth-century Khazars to the "holy household" of Reformation Augsburg.[1]

How, then, to chart the new topography? The household, legitimate sexual union, and fertility now lie in the shadow of an otherworldly ideal, one that asks men and women to think of themselves as autonomous, detachable individuals with a spiritual fate independent of kin or class. It is this idea of a human identity scaled down to the level of the individual which Christianity borrows from the ancient romance and which will reach toward the introspective self-consciousness so cherished in the western tradition. It is because of the monumental place this postclassical notion of the individual holds for us that we are often unable to grasp the centrality of group and dynasty to the ancient sense of human identity.[2]

This raises obstacles for the study of gender in antiquity, because we tend to be deaf to the anxieties of a population whose idea of authentic identity was bound to enactment—performance—of the self in community, and whose idea of community included not only the living but even the dead. No ancient person, male or female, would have had an inkling of what we moderns value in an idea of individualism or personal autonomy. Even to reject the group was a gesture within the group consciousness.

Women, we have seen, were understood as the supreme guardians of the household. When they were spoken of, when they spoke themselves, it was not as autonomous social agents but as arbiters of morality for the kin group. This may help to explain why both the bride, the figure of concord, and the more disruptive figure of the virgin both drew on women's long-accepted roles within the household, whether as wife or—in the case of the virgin—as sister and daughter.[3] Among Christians, both traditionalist and separatist women claimed this continuity where they could: traditionalists by asserting the Christian dimension of their wifely function, separatists by elaborating on their capacity as daughter and sister, substituting continence for chastity as the sign of sexual virtue.

Women's class status was complicated by gender. Yet modern historians have often failed to perceive that the elite women documented by the vast majority of our sources would not have seen themselves as without recourse to power, however much they felt their power was compromised by gender. The same woman could perceive herself as both low-status and high-status depending on context. If her position was subordinate to that of other, male age-peers within her family ranking, in the world beyond the family her claim was that of rank and not of gender. Then again, in the case of high-ranking women, an emphasis on a woman's subordinate position within the household might serve as a play on the disjunction between high family status and low status within the family. But to speak as the moral voice of an elite *domus* was to hold a position of real power.

Beneath all these rich ambiguities, what all aristocratic men and women shared was a moral language that turned on the notion of reluctance. The gesture of reluctance to power was not, of course, an actual refusal: rather, it was a signal of good intentions, a guarantee that the power conferred would be used for the common good and not to a personal end. In any event, it should be remembered that the language of reluctance to power was a moral language used less by the powerless than by the powerful. When women disclaimed an interest in the public sphere, it was usually a sign that they had already calculated the public outcome of their "private" actions.

The introduction of the virginal ideal led to a tense coexistence between two versions of this symbolic language. Though a certain strand of early Christian literature attempted to supplant the wife by the virgin, the historical result was more ambiguous. Each was a figure both of female reluctance and of female power. The symbolic reign of the wife, the guarantor of *concordia,* had contributed to social stasis by its emphasis on regeneration and dynasty, the household and the city. The introduction of the figure of the virgin, the daughter who refused to pass from her initial role within one household to that of the wife in another, offered a new model of moral authenticity, one that classical society would have rejected as opening the way symbolically for other antisocial actions but one that, after a struggle, late Roman society accepted with enthusiasm. It may be argued that the Christian writers of antiquity introduced the ideal of the virgin precisely because of her paradoxical quality: as a rhetorical figure, she invoked the conservative values of the hearth while in fact legitimizing social change.

What remains to be understood is how the introduction of this new figure of female reluctance and authority changed the symbolic and moral economy of the Roman Mediterranean at the end of antiquity. Those who claimed her as their moral guarantor derived a new advantage in the competition for civic authority. But her arrival may also have changed the terms of the contest itself, by abetting the kind of absolute claim to moral authenticity that the earlier system had been designed to foreclose. It is still too early to know what a searching gender-based analysis of late Roman modes of identity and authority can tell us about the end of the classical world: this study is only a prologue. What is clear is that, as a rhetorical figure, the virgin was more volatile than the bride, both because of her ambiguity and because her arrival disrupted the old moral language of *concordia.*

We can no longer afford the luxury of inattention to such complexities. Our own century has seen a shift in the rhetorical economy of gender as profound as that of the late Roman period. Although both virgin and bride remain as elements in our cultural imagination, their symbolic function in reinforcing women's position as mobilizers of consensus within a kin group is increasingly perceived by western elites as degrading to women—a development intimately linked to the erosion of the kin group as the central social, economic, and political unit. But one of the most powerful variations of the Christian ascetic heroine, the heroine trapped in the *domus* of wrong-minded male kin, has if anything a growing significance as one strand of western society progressively invests the individual with precedence over the household as the locus of moral authenticity, while another strand of this society, accompanied by much of the rest of the world, invokes the moral language of "family values"—a traditionalism far removed in spirit from that of Roman intellectuals both pagan and Christian.

This is a fact of alarming importance in the postcolonial world order. While a charge of misogyny is regularly weighed against traditionalist elements of western and postcolonial societies alike, conversely an ideal of female reluctance in the public sphere becomes one of the vehicles by which traditionalists assert their autonomy from and resentment of western cultural elites.[4] A contest over who has the right to speak for the heroine hidden, or trapped, within the household becomes a contest over the right to appropriate her authority as a figure of wronged vulnerability.

What will result from the introduction of the ideological heroine into the debate between western humanist elites and their fundamentalist critics is uncertain, but the recourse to such a figure should be greeted with caution. We have seen that her magnetism can have far-reaching and in some cases destructive consequences. That these consequences for antiquity are not yet fully understood means that their implications for modernity are similarly—perhaps dangerously—unclear. In the case of late antiquity, her authority seems to have favored the purveyors of what a modern humanist might call religious extremism, at the expense of the pluralist sensibility of Roman traditionalists. Whether the same will be true in our own day depends in part on the degree of attention we lend to the volatile role of gender in the discourse of moral superiority, and in particular to the rhetorical meanings we allow to the *pathos* of a heroine. As we turn from the past to the future, we should beware the allure of a figure who still moves among us.

· Abbreviations ·

AASS	*Acta Sanctorum*
AB	*Analecta Bollandiana*
BHG	*Bibliotheca Hagiographica Graeca*
BHL	*Bibliotheca Hagiographica Latina*
CC	*Corpus Christianorum (Series Latina)*
CIL	*Corpus Inscriptionum Latinarum*
CSEL	*Corpus Scriptorum Ecclesiasticorum Latinorum*
GCN	*Groningen Colloquia on the Novel*
ILS	*Inscriptiones Latinae Selectae*
JEH	*Journal of Ecclesiastical History*
JRS	*Journal of Roman Studies*
PG	*Patrologia Graeca*
PL	*Patrologia Latina*
PLRE	*Prosopography of the Later Roman Empire*
PLS	*Patrologia Latina—Supplementum*
RB	*Revue Bénédictine*
REAug	*Revue des Etudes Augustiniennes*
SC	*Sources Chrétiennes*

· Notes ·

1. Private Lives, Public Meanings

1. Veyne, "La famille et l'amour sous le haut-empire romain" (1978), 37.

2. But see Richard Saller, "Corporal Punishment, Authority, and Obedience in the Roman Household" (1991).

3. Veyne has been criticized for neglecting the evidence for affective relationships in families in the Republican period discussed by Saller and Shaw, "Tombstones and Roman Family Relations in the Principate" (1984).

4. Especially vol. 3, *Le souci de soi* (1984).

5. On the substantial secondary literature responding to Veyne and Foucault, see Bremmer, "Why Did Early Christianity Attract Upper-Class Women?" (1989), 45nn20–21, and Cameron, "Redrawing the Map" (1986), 266–271.

6. Benabou, "Pratique matrimoniale et représentation philosophique" (1987), argues that the Stoic emphasis on marriage as a sharing of life (e.g. Musonius Rufus, *Reliquiae* 13A) emerged not because of changes in aristocratic family relations but because the Stoics championed marriage in order to silence the Epicureans.

7. Levick, "Concordia at Rome" (1978), characterizes the propaganda of concord as a binding of men through the conjugal bond: "*concordia augusta* became the harmony between the princeps and his wife (or mother), who embodied the deity as the female link between the princeps and his male kinsmen" (227). On the visual media, see Kampen, "Between Public and Private" (1991).

8. See e.g. the collection of essays, *Il matrimonio nella società altomedievale* (1977).

9. See e.g. Shelton, "Pliny the Younger and the Ideal Wife" (1990), on Foucault's neglect of the experience and self-representation of women in his discussion of ancient marriage. The state of affairs more broadly is well summarized, with a thorough bibliography, in Richlin, "The Ethnographer's Dilemma and the Dream of a Lost Golden Age" (1993).

10. Plutarch, *Praecepta coniugalia* 140D.

11. For a critical overview of recent scholarship on the *Erōtikos*, see Brenk, "Plutarch's *Erotikos:* The Drag Down Pulled Up" (1988). For an alternate and complementary view, see Cooper, "Insinuations of Womanly Influence" (1992), and Goldhill, *Foucault's Virginity* (1995), 144ff.

12. The irony here also casts light on Plutarch's view of two important questions of the time: whether the wise man should marry and whether, within marriage, sex for pleasure (as opposed to procreation) is licit. Both are discussed in Van Geytenbeek, *Musonius Rufus and Greek Diatribe* (1962), 67ff, 71ff.

13. See Flacelière, ed., *Dialogue sur l'amour* (1980), 13–14, on the identity of Plutarch in the dialogue.

14. *Life of Pompey*, 2.10. It is disputed whether *epi tais gametais* refers to affairs with married women or to Pompey's own successive wives; the latter reading seems possible in light of my discussion.

15. See Plutarch, *Life of Caesar*, 1.1, for an instance in which Sulla attempted to exact the same kind of allegiance from Caesar, who refused.

16. The first few paragraphs of this section summarize an argument put forward in greater detail in Cooper, "Insinuations of Womanly Influence."

17. *De civitate dei* 5.15 (*CSEL* 40.242).

18. Winkler, *The Constraints of Desire* (1990), 50.

19. See Boatwright, "Plancia Magna of Perge: Women's Roles and Status in Roman Asia Minor" (1991), esp. 262ff.

20. Austin, *How to Do Things with Words* (1962). Goffman, *The Presentation of Self in Everyday Life* (1959), and *Frame Analysis* (1974).

21. For a guide to the various subfields of discourse analysis, see Schiffrin, *Approaches to Discourse* (1994).

22. Davies and Harré, "Positioning" (1990), 45.

23. For a window onto the culture of public speech in late antiquity, see Kaster, *Guardians of Language* (1988), Bartsch, *Actors in the Audience* (1994), and Gleason, *Making Men* (1995).

24. Van Ommeslaeghe, "Jean Chrysostome en conflit avec l'impératrice Eudoxie" (1979); van Ommeslaeghe draws the account of Martyrius from MS Graecus 1519, Bibliothèque Nationale, Paris.

25. Palladius, *Dialogue on the Life of John Chrysostom*, 8 (*SC* 341.178).

26. Ibid., 7 (*SC* 341.162). cf. Holum, *Theodosian Empresses* (1982), 74n105, who interprets Palladius in light of the later traditions.

27. MS Graecus 1519, 506b, cited in van Ommeslaeghe, 153. My translation is from van Ommeslaeghe's quotation (in French) from the MS.

28. Two undated homilies, *Homilia ante exilium* (*PG* 52.427–432) and *Homilia cum iret in exilium* (*PG* 52.435–438), bearing in the manuscripts a dubious

attribution to Chrysostom, both listed in Aldema, *Repertorium Pseudochrysostomicum* (1965), nn422 and 528, as of uncertain authorship, used material from Martyrius to vivify a tradition that Martyrius did not himself record, that John had railed against Eudoxia as Jezebel (van Ommeslaeghe, 157). *Homilia ante exilium* (*PG* 52.431): "The seed of Jezebel is still with us . . . But bring on the wondrous and resourceful herald of life, John [the Baptist], that is, a poor man, who, while he possessed not even a candle, still possessed the lamp of Christ. Eve's helpmate coveted his head!"

29. Thus, the rhetorical element of womanly influence could operate simultaneously at two levels and in two directions. John was accused of being incited by Eudoxia to ire, even as he accused Arcadius of letting his wife control his affairs (the force of the Biblical allusions).

2. The Ancient Novel

1. Proem to *Daphnis and Chloe,* tr. Gill, in Reardon, *Collected Ancient Greek Novels* (1989), 288–289. (Cited translations of novels are from this volume.)

2. See e.g. Konstan, *Sexual Symmetry* (1994).

3. See e.g. Elsom, "Callirhoe: Displaying the Phallic Woman" (1992).

4. Reardon, *Novels,* 2.

5. For an overview of dating, see ibid., 5ff.

6. Merkelbach, *Roman und Mysterium in der Antike* (1962).

7. Perry, *The Ancient Romances* (1967), 30ff.

8. Scholars of early Christian literature have for some decades been alive to the connection: Söder, *Die apokryphen Apostelgeschichte und die romanhafte Literatur der Antike* (1932), and more recently Perkins, "The Apocryphal Acts and the Early Christian Martyrdom" (1985), and Pervo, *Profit with Delight* (1987).

9. As an illustration of the broad problem of understanding the readership of ancient texts, consider the controversy provoked by W. V. Harris' *Ancient Literacy* (1989): e.g. *Literacy in the Roman World* (1991). Bagnall's "An Owner of Literary Papyri" (1992) offers a concrete approach to the problem in its analysis of the library of Aurelia Ptolemais, a matron of Oxyrhynchus in the late third century.

10. Egger, "Zu den Frauenrollen im griechischen Roman" (1988). See also Wesseling, "The Audience of the Ancient Novels" (1988); Stephens, "Who Read the Ancient Novels?" (1994); Bowie, "The Readership of Greek Novels in the Ancient World" (1994).

11. Anderson, *Eros Sophistes* (1982).

12. Goldhill, *Foucault's Virginity* (1995).

13. Peter Brown's paraphrase of Musonius Rufus, Fragment 14, in his *The Body and Society* (1988), 5, 8.

14. Cf. Nightingale, "The Folly of Praise" (1993).

15. On the date of the *Erōtes*, see Buffière, *Eros adolescent* (1980), 481, arguing for a late second-century date. See also Halperin, "Historicizing the Sexual Body" (1992).

16. Pseudo-Lucian, *Erōtes* 14.

17. *Leukippe and Kleitophon*, 2.35–38 (tr. Winkler, in Reardon, *Novels*, 205–208).

18. *Chaereas and Callirhoe*, 1.1 (tr. Reardon, 22).

19. See Egger, "Women and Marriage in the Greek Novels" (1994).

20. Winkler, "The Education of Chloe: Hidden Injuries of Sex," in his *Constraints of Desire* (1990), 101–126; Zeitlin, "The Poetics of *Erōs*" (1990).

21. On the female slave's legal standing vis-à-vis her owner's disposition of her sexual favors, see Sicari, *Prostituzione e tutela giuridica della schiava* (1991).

22. *Leukippe and Kleitophon*, 21 (tr. Winkler, 259).

23. The resemblance is noted in Shaw, "The Passion of Perpetua" (1993), 9.

24. See Burrus, "Reading Agnes" (1995), on the pornographic quality of similar scenes in the martyr literature and elsewhere.

25. Bartsch, *Decoding the Ancient Novel* (1989).

26. See e.g. Dawson, *Allegorical Readers and Cultural Revision in Ancient Alexandria* (1992); Lamberton, *Homer the Theologian* (1986); MacDonald, *Christianizing Homer* (1994).

27. Winkler, *Auctor and Actor* (1985).

28. On marriage contracts, see Treggiari, *Roman Marriage* (1991), chap. 3, "Choosing a *Coniunx*," and chap. 4, "From Negotiation to Engagement."

29. For Konstan's argument that this shift in literary form is itself a response to the cultural decentering of empire, see "The Invention of Fiction" (1993).

30. Graham Anderson, *Ancient Fiction* (1984).

31. See Felson-Rubin, *Regarding Penelope* (1994).

32. Garnsey, "Aspects of the Decline of the Urban Aristocracy in the Empire" (1974), 241.

33. Reardon, *Novels*, 7.

34. Musonius Rufus, *Reliphiae* 15B, cited in Hopkins, *Death and Renewal* (1983), 96.

35. On the suspicion attending claims to ascetic virtue, see Francis, *Subversive Virtue* (1995).

36. See Raditsa, "Augustus' Legislation" (1980).

3. "The Bride That Is No Bride"

1. *Passion of Andrew,* 37 (5) (MacDonald, 375). The reconstruction of the Greek *Acts of Andrew* followed here, from a diversity of fragmentary ancient sources, is drawn from MacDonald, *The Acts of Andrew and the Acts of Andrew and Matthias in the City of the Cannibals* (1990). Throughout I cite Mac-Donald's translation, which appears in the same volume.

2. Xenocharides and Leonidas are remembered in a letter of Pope Innocent I to Exuperius of Toulouse, *Epistula* 6.7.13 (*PL* 20.502). For discussion of the evidence, see MacDonald, *Acts of Andrew,* 48ff.

3. For discussion of the date and context of the Apocryphal Acts, see Schnee-melcher's introduction in his *New Testament Apocrypha* (1992), 75–86.

4. *Passion of Andrew,* 1 (MacDonald, 327).

5. Gregory of Tours, *Liber de miraculis beati Andreae apostoli* 30, as supplemented by MacDonald, 309.

6. *Acta Petris* 33(4) (in Lipsius and Bonnet, *Acta Apostolorum Apocrypha* [1891], 1.84).

7. *Acta Pauli* 7 (Lipsius-Bonnet, 1.240).

8. *Acta Ioannis* 19 (in Lipsius and Bonnet, *Acta Apostolorum Apocrypha* [1898], 2.1.161): Lycomedes is "a wealthy man, who was praetor of the Ephesians." In Gregory of Tours' *Liber de miraculis* 30 (MacDonald, 306–307), Maximilla of Patras is "the proconsul's wife."

9. See *Liber de miraculis* 30 for the healing of Maximilla (MacDonald, 308–311). For the conversion to continence, see *Passion of Andrew* 14 (MacDonald, 342ff).

10. *Acta Ioannis* 19 (Lipsius-Bonnet, 2.1.161).

11. Papyrus Oxyrhyncus 850, discussed in Schäferdiek, "The Acts of John" (1992), 157. See also Schäferdiek, "The Manichaean Collection of Apocryphal Acts Ascribed to Leucius Charinus" (1992), 88.

12. *Acta Thomae* 94 (in Lipsius and Bonnet, *Acta Apostolorum Apocrypha* [1903], 2.2.207, 240ff). Mygdonia refuses to sleep with Charisius on account of illness (*Acta Thomae* 89 [Lipsius-Bonnet, 2.2.204]). Tertia's exhortation to Misdaeus to "keep yourself holy to the living God" (*Acta Thomae* 137 [Lipsius-Bonnet, 2.2.244]) is intended in the same spirit.

13. Thamyris, Thecla's betrothed, is "the first man of the city": *Acta Pauli* 11 (Lipsius-Bonnet, 1.243). Alexander, who falls in love with her and causes her near martyrdom in Antioch, appears in certain versions of the text as "one of the first of the Antiochenes" (26; variants in Lipsius-Bonnet, 1.253).

14. See e.g. Janssens, *Vita e morte del cristiano negli epitaffi di Roma* (1981).

15. Following Burrus, *Chastity as Autonomy: Women in the Stories of Apocryphal Acts* (1987), although she herself notes (2n4) that indiscriminate use of the term "chastity" might lead to confusion.

16. *Vita Syncleticae* 24 (*PG* 28.1501).

17. Söder, *Die apokryphen Apostelgeschichten,* 216.

18. MacDonald, *The Legend and the Apostle* (1983), 17ff.

19. Tertullian, *De baptismo* 17 (*CC* 1.291).

20. As in 1 Corinthians 16.19; Romans 16.3ff; Acts 18.18.

21. Theissen, *The Sociology of Early Palestinian Christianity* (1978).

22. Douglas, "Social Preconditions of Enthusiasm and Heterodoxy" (1969), 71. See discussion in Gager, "Body-Symbols and Social Reality" (1982), 347.

23. Francis, *Subversive Virtue* (1995), xvii.

24. Valantasis, "A Theory of the Social Function of Asceticism" (1995), 548.

25. Averil Cameron has written compellingly on this new language in *Christianity and the Rhetoric of Empire* (1991).

26. Tannen, *You Just Don't Understand* (1991), 290–291.

27. Jean-Jacques Rousseau, *The Social Contract* 4.8, tr. Maurice Cranston (Harmondsworth: Penguin, 1968), 178–179.

28. Chang, *Wild Swans* (1991), offers a peasant's view of the situation.

29. A western journalist, who queried Lee Kuan Yew, the leader of the People's Action Party and former prime minister of Singapore, about Singapore's sole political prisoner, records a brusque response: "I also asked Lee about Chia Thye Poh—how a man so modest and considerate could be seen as a threat. As I described Chia's qualities, Lee interrupted, saying, 'Chinese Communist style. That is the ideal communist. You must be humble, you must be very frugal and Spartan, not flashy, not trying to awe or impress people. *They* impress people by their humility and self-sacrificing manner, a certain exaggerated understatement of themselves, but a steely determination.' " Sesser, *The Lands of Charm and Cruelty* (1994), 48.

30. See e.g. MacMullen, *Corruption and the Decline of Rome* (1988).

31. I take the phrase from Kaestli, "Response [to Virginia Burrus]" (1986), 119, where the relevant scholarship is summarized. For more recent bibliography, and a perspective differing significantly from mine, see Boughton, "From Pious Legend to Feminist Fantasy" (1991).

32. Davies, *The Revolt of the Widows* (1980), 86.

33. See e.g. Kaestli, "Fiction littéraire et réalité sociale" (1990), and Dunn, "Women's Liberation, the *Acts of Paul,* and other Apocryphal Acts of the Apostles" (1993).

34. Nock, *Conversion* (1933); Kraemer, "The Conversion of Women to Ascetic Forms of Christianity" (1980).

35. MacDonald, *The Legend and the Apostle*, 54ff.

36. E.g. *Adversus haereses* 1.13.3 (*PG* 7.581–586). On the idea in ancient literature from Plato to Sozomen "that women were especially given to silly religious ideas and experiences," see MacMullen, *Christianizing the Roman Empire* (1984), 9n33.

37. On widows and old women, see Bremmer, "Pauper or Patroness" (1995).

38. Origen, *Contra Celsum* 6.34 (*PG* 11.1349), quoted in Cameron, *Christianity and the Rhetoric of Empire*, 89.

39. See Cooper, "Insinuations of Womanly Influence," 158ff.

40. Tertullian, *De baptismo* 1.17 (*CC* 1.291). Souter, "The 'Acta Pauli' etc. in Tertullian" (1924), 292, records a textual variant of the passage which mentions the *Acts of Paul* explicitly. See discussion in MacDonald, *The Legend and the Apostle*, 17ff.

41. Culler, "Readers and Reading: Reading as a Woman," in his *On Deconstruction* (1982), 43–64.

42. See Radway, *Reading the Romance* (1984), for modern fieldwork on reading for identity.

4. An Angel in the House

1. Jerome, *Epistula* 39.6 (*CSEL* 54.306).

2. *Epistula* 45 (*CSEL* 54.323–329). He seems to have been formally banned in August 385; in any case, he left Rome in that month. See Kelly, *Jerome* (1975), 111ff.

3. Epistula 22.41 (*CSEL* 54.209).

4. *Vita Macrinae* 2 (*PG* 46.961).

5. Pseudo-Basil, *Homilia de virginitate* 99–101, text in Amand and Moons, "Une curieuse homélie grecque inédite sur la virginité" (1953), 59–60. Amand and Moons propose an early fourth-century date for the text, but on generic grounds that is a half-century or more too early. The translation here is by Teresa M. Shaw in Wimbush, *Ascetic Behavior in Greco-Roman Antiquity* (1990), 39–40.

6. On the dating, see Clark, *The Life of Melania the Younger* (1984), 17–24.

7. See Clark, "The Life of Melania the Younger and the Hellenistic Romance: A Genre Exploration," ibid., 153–170.

8. Jerome, *Epistula* 127.5 (*CSEL* 56.149). Gordini, "Origine e sviluppo del monachesimo a Roma" (1956), 224.

9. Jerome, *Epistula* 22.15 (*CSEL* 54.162): "prima Romanae urbis virgo nobilis esse coepisti."

10. Although the evidence on asceticism in Rome before Marcella is uncertain, Gordini suggests (231–232) that one might argue for the existence of virgins there by analogy from Carthage (and elsewhere).

11. The seminal text is Ruether, "Misogynism and Virginal Feminism in the Fathers of the Church" (1974). See also Clark, "Ascetic Renunciation and Feminine Advancement" (1981).

12. Brooten, "Jewish Women's History in the Roman Period" (1986). See also Kellenbach, *Anti-Judaism in Feminist Religious Writings* (1994).

13. As exemplified in Coventry Patmore's popular poem sequence, *The Angel in the House* (1854). On the iconic quality of female virtue, see Casteras, *Images of Victorian Womanhood in English Art* (1987).

14. *Codex Theodosianus* 8.16.1 (31 January 320).

15. Ibid. 16.2.1 (31 October 313) and 16.2.2 (21 October 319); 1.27.1 (23 June 318).

16. Brown, *Power and Persuasion in Late Antiquity* (1988), chap. 3, "Poverty and Power."

17. A point made in Frend, *The Rise of Christianity* (1984), 489.

18. See McLynn, *Ambrose of Milan* (1994), chap. 1, "The Reluctant Bishop."

19. Ammianus Marcellinus, *Res gestae* 16.8.12.

20. Ibid. 27.11.1. Ambrose owed his standing as governor (*consularis*) to the patronage of the same Petronius Probus (McLynn, *Ambrose of Milan,* 39ff).

21. Vernant, "Hestia-Hermes," in *Myth and Thought among the Greeks* (1983), 127–175. Beard, "The Sexual Status of Vestal Virgins" (1980).

22. This diminished role of women is a point made by Consolino, "Modelli di comportamento," in Giardina (1986), 273–306. On the variety of roles, see Kraemer, *Her Share of the Blessings* (1992).

23. The issues of method have been discussed particularly with reference to Judaism in the Roman period. See Brooten, *Women Leaders in the Ancient Synagogue* (1982), and Rajak and Noy, "*Archisynagogoi*" (1993).

24. Two recent and very different accounts of the emergence of female asceticism as a vehicle for female authority are Elm, *Virgins of God* (1994), and Cloke, *"This Female Man of God"* (1995).

25. See Martimort, *Les diaconesses* (1982).

26. Ambrose, *De virginitate* 6.34 (*PL* 16.288).

27. See e.g. Consolino, "Dagli *exempla* ad un esempio di comportamento cristiano" (1982), and her *"Veni huc a Libano"* (1984).

28. Jerome, *Epistula* 107.1 (*CSEL* 55.291). Albinus is Laeta's father, Publilius Caeonius Caecina Albinus; Laeta had married Paula's son Toxotius, and the child in question is their newborn daughter, also named Paula.

29. Pelagius, *Epistula ad Demetriadem* 2 (*PL* 30.16).

30. Pseudo-Jerome, *De virginitate* 12 (*PL* 30.178).

31. Gordini, "Origine e sviluppo del monachesimo," 259–260.

32. Hunter, "Resistance to the Virginal Ideal in Late Fourth-Century Rome" (1987). See also his "Helvidius, Jovinianm and the Virginity of Mary in Late Fourth-Century Rome" (1993).

33. On social class, see Clark, "Authority and Humility" (1985).

34. Scott, *Gender and the Politics of History* (1989).

35. Throughout what follows I have retained the word *matrona* in Latin, both to distinguish it from *uxor*, here rendered as "wife," and to signal the ambiguity of its meaning, which the English "matron" does not precisely render. Technically, a *matrona* can be any married female citizen, but from the republic onwards, the term also connotes high social standing.

36. Majorian, *Novellae* 6 (26 October 458).

37. Rufinus, *Apologia* 2.6–7 (*CC* 20.87–88).

38. Cameron, "Paganism and Literature in Late Fourth-Century Rome" (1977), 23–24. On Virgil, see also Courcelle, *Lecteurs païens et lecteurs chrétiens de l'Enéide* (1984).

39. See Murphy, *Rufinus of Aquileia* (1945), 119ff, for historical background on Rufinus' version of the *Sentences of Sextus* and his relationship to Avita, to whom the translation is dedicated, and her husband Apronianus.

40. Jerome, *Epistula* 133.3 (*CSEL* 56.246–247). I have followed the vivid translation of this passage by Henry Chadwick in *The Sentences of Sextus* (1959), 120.

41. *Adversus Jovinianum* 1.49 (*PL* 23.281), quoting maxim 231.

42. *Commentarii in Ezechielem* 6.18 (*PL* 25.173).

5. The Whispering Critics at Blesilla's Funeral

1. George Eliot, *Adam Bede* (Harmondsworth: Penguin, 1985), 113.

2. On the Proiecta casket, see Shelton, *The Esquiline Treasure* (1981).

3. An unpublished manuscript by Ann Kuttner of the University of Pennsylvania documents the continuity of Venus imagery from Augustus to Justinian.

4. On "civic" and "sectarian" Christianity in the fourth and fifth centuries, see Limberis, *Divine Heiress* (1994).

5. Jerome, *Epistula* 39.6 (*CSEL* 54.306).

6. All quotations from Aphthonius, *Progymnasmata* 13 (tr. Nadeau, 281).

7. Consolino, "Modelli di comportamento," 284ff.

8. Hunter, "Resistance to the Virginal Ideal" (1987), 55. See also Tiblietti, *Verginità e matrimonio in antichi scrittori cristiani* (1983), 60ff, on the connec-

tion between the repudiation of marriage and of the Hebrew Bible in the writings of Clement of Alexandria and Tertullian against the Marcionites.

9. According to Jerome, *Adversus Helvidium* 18 (*PL* 23.202). Kelly, *Jerome* (1975), 105, traces the anti-Manichaean elements in Helvidius' argument.

10. See Van Geytenbeek, *Musonius Rufus and Greek Diatribe* (1962), 67ff.

11. Jerome, *Adversus Jovinianum* 1.46 (*PL* 23.275). See Markus, *The End of Ancient Christianity* (1990), esp. chap. 4, "Augustine: A Defence of Christian Mediocrity," 45ff.

12. Jerome, *Epistula* 49.13 (*CSEL* 54.368).

13. On the circumstances of the stele's production, see Polara, "Le iscrizioni sul cippo tombale di Vezzio Agorio Pretestato" (1967). Similar inscriptions are preserved, such as that of Tetratia Isias and C. Sosius Julianus discussed in Festugière, "Initiée par l'époux" (1967).

14. See Bloch, "The Pagan Revival in the West at the End of the Fourth Century" (1963). Cameron, "Paganism and Literature in Late Fourth-Century Rome" (1977), challenges the evidence for a full-scale pagan revival, but the importance of Praetextatus is not in doubt. The quotation is from Matthews, "Symmachus and the Oriental Cults" (1973), 179.

15. *ILS* 1259, C1–12.

16. See Kirkby, "The Scholar and His Public" (1981).

17. Symmachus, *Epistula* 2.36.3.

18. Consolino, "Modelli di comportamento," 284.

19. Cracco Ruggini, *Il paganesimo romano tra religione e politica* (1979).

20. *Carmen contra paganos,* lines 9–13 (*PLS* 1.781).

21. Matthews, "The Historical Setting of the 'Carmen contra paganos' " (1970), 472, commenting on lines 26 and 27. Although I have illustrated the connection to Jerome's response to Paulina from Matthews' study, Matthews himself does not accept Praetextatus as the prefect in the *Carmen*.

22. The invective would have seemed particularly inappropriate if Martindale and Jones are correct in implying that Paula and Eustochium were related to Praetextatus by marriage. They identify Praetextata, the wife of Iulius Festus Hymetius (who, as the brother of Iulius Toxotius, was Paula's brother-in-law and Eustochium's uncle), as a relative, possibly a sister, of Vettius Agorius Praetextatus (*PLRE* 1.721). She appears in Jerome's *Epistula* 107.5 (*CSEL* 55.296) as a pagan attempting to interest the girl in fine dresses.

23. *CIL* 6.1756, tr. Croke and Harries, *Religious Conflict in Fourth-Century Rome* (1982), 117.

24. For the relationship between Secundus and Apronianus, see Cameron, "The Date and Owners of the Esquiline Treasure" (1985), and Shelton, "The Esquiline Treasure" (1985).

25. Rufinus, *Praefatio* to Origen's *Homiliae in Psalmos 36–38* (*CC* 20.251).

26. The paraphrase is by Murphy, *Rufinus* (1945), 111.

27. Rufinus, *Praefatio, Sententiae Sixti* (*CC* 20.259).

28. See Beatrice, *Tradux Peccati* (1978), and Markus, *End of Ancient Christianity,* esp. chaps. 4, 5.

29. I have accepted the attribution made by Robert Evans, *Four Letters of Pelagius* (1968), but the possibility that the *Ad Celantiam* was written by a later writer, with reference to Pelagius' *Ad Demetriadem* and Augustine's Letter 262 to Ecdicia, should not be dismissed out of hand and would not substantially alter my argument.

30. Augustine, *Epistula* 262.3 (*CSEL* 52.623).

31. Further discussion of this question as it appears in Letter 262 can be found in Cooper, "Insinuations of Womanly Influence," 158ff.

32. On the date of the *Ad Celantiam,* see Evans, *Four Letters,* 22.

33. On grounds of internal evidence, the text could plausibly be dated as early as the beginning of the fifth century or as late as the end of the sixth. See Cooper, "Concord and Martyrdom" (1993), appendix B, "The Date and Authorship of the *Liber ad Gregoriam."*

34. The only substantial published treatment of the *Liber* is a valuable but in many respects misleading article by Morin, "Un traité inédit d'Arnobe le Jeune" (1910). For an English translation of the text, see Cooper, "Concord and Martyrdom," appendix A.

35. Markus, *End of Ancient Christianity,* 82.

36. Karlsruhe, Landesbibliothek, Bib. Aug. 172 (saec. IX); the manuscript is discussed in Beccaria, *I codici miniati del periodo presalernitano* (1956). The explicit is recorded in Holder, *Die Reichenauer Handschriften* (1906), 1.405.

37. Romans 11.33; Psalms 125.5; James 1.2–4; Romans 5.3–5; John 16.20–22.

38. *Liber ad Gregoriam* 1 (*PLS* 3.222).

39. A comparison may be drawn to the vision from a tower of Benedict of Nursia recorded in *Dialogue* 2.35 of Gregory the Great (*SC* 260.236–242). See Courcelle, "La vision cosmique de S. Benoît" (1967), who discusses in detail the symbolic function of the tower.

40. Cf. Romans 12.1–2: "I entreat you by the mercy of our Lord Jesus Christ, that you seek to know what is the will of God, what is just and good, and what perfect," cited at *Liber ad Gregoriam* 17 (*PLS* 3.241); and Psalms 118.4.

41. Morin, "Fragments pélagiens inédits du manuscrit 954 de Vienne" (1922).

42. Gregory of Nyssa, *Vita Macrinae* 2 (*PG* 46.961); Jerome, *Epistula* 22.41 (*CSEL* 54.209). The relevant sections of Athanasius' treatise are preserved in

the Armenian version edited by Casey, "Der dem Athanasius zugeschriebene Traktat, *Peri parthenías*" (1935), 1034. Pseudo-Basil, *Homilia de virginitate* 99–101 in Amand and Moons (1953).

43. John the Faster, *Sermo de poenitentia* (*PG* 88.1969).

44. *Vita Olympiadis* 1.24–7 (*SC* 13 bis.408).

45. Aubineau, "Panégyrique de Thècle attribué à Jean Chrysostome" (1975), 352.

46. Augustine, *De sancta virginitate* 45 (*CSEL* 41.290).

47. *Vita Syncleticae* 8 (*PG* 28.1489–92), tr. Castelli, in Wimbush, *Ascetic Behavior*, 260–270. On Syncletica, see Castelli, "Mortifying the Body, Curing the Soul" (1992).

48. Jerome's catalogue of "mulieres romanae insignes" appears at *Adversus Jovinianum* 1.46 (*PL* 23.275).

49. *Acta Matthaei* (*BHL* 5691) 2.17 (*Acta Sanctorum Sept. VI*, 233).

50. *Liber ad Gregoriam* 4 (*PLS* 3.225).

51. See e.g. Augustine, Letter 262 to Ecdicia (*CSEL* 57.621–631).

52. See Markus, *End of Ancient Christianity*, chap. 4, "Augustine: A Defence of Christian Mediocrity," 45ff.

53. On the vast literature tracing fourth-century asceticism back to the pre-Constantinian martyrs, see e.g. Van Loveren, "Once Again" (1982).

6. The Imprisoned Heroine

1. Dufourcq, *Etude sur les Gesta Martyrum romains* (1988), 1.334ff. On Rome under Leo, see McShane, *La romanitas et le pape Léon le Grand* (1979).

2. Consolino, "Modelli di santità" (1984), discusses the primary texts and secondary literature with characteristic thoroughness.

3. On the martyr cult in Rome, see Alchermes, "*Cura pro mortuis* and *cultus martyrum*" (1989).

4. Vauchez, "Saints admirables et saints imitables" (1991).

5. We know that the *Gesta* were intended for liturgical use from the prologue to the *Passio Anastasiae;* the text is in Delehaye, *Etude sur le legendier Romain* (1936) *les saints de novembre et de décembre* (Brussels: Société des Bollandistes, 1936)(Subsidia Hagiographica, 23), 221–249; here, 222. See also de Gaiffier, "Un prologue hagiographique hostile au décret de Gélase?" (1964).

6. Jerome, *Adversus Jovinianum* 2.2 (*PL* 23.284).

7. Augustine, *Contra Faustum* 20.21 (*PL* 42.384–385).

8. Schäferdiek, "The Manichaean Collection" (1992), 88.

9. Evodius, *De fide contra Manichaeos* 38 (*PL* 42.1150).

10. Monachesi, "Arnobio il Giovane ed una sua possibile attività agiografica," (1922), 124, suggests a common authorship for the two documents; de Gaiffier,

"Un prologue hostile" (347n2), follows Germain Morin in concluding that the author of the *Liber ad Gregoriam* knew the *Passio Anastasiae*.

11. Other married women martyrs known and venerated in Rome are commemorated in surviving *gesta* of their own, notably Felicitas (*BHL* 2853) and Symphorosa (*BHL* 7971), who are both mentioned briefly in the *Liber ad Gregoriam*.

12. Lenain de Tillemont, *Mémoires pour servir à l'histoire ecclésiastique des six premiers siècles* (1698), 323.

13. Augustine, *Epistula* 262.4 (*CSEL* 57.624). On the humility of her attire, see sec. 9 (*CSEL* 57.629).

14. As in *Acta Ioannis* 63 (Lipsius-Bonnet, 2.1.181–182), where Drusiana is shut into a tomb by her husband Andronicus.

15. *Passio Anastasiae* 2 (Delehaye, 223).

16. Bilinkoff, "Woman with a Mission" (1994), illuminates the issue of frustration for a later period.

17. For an interesting parallel to the *Passio*'s interest in self-understanding, see the stress on the importance to Christian progress of hope—and of a self-understanding that protects against discouragement—in Pelagius' *Epistula ad Demetriadem* 2 (*PL* 30.16).

18. On Cassian's *Conferences*, see Leyser, "*Lectio divina, oratio pura*" (1994).

19. Cassian, *Conlationes* 14.9 (*SC* 54.194–195).

20. David Konstan, "Frankness, Flattery, and Friendship" (1992).

21. Rousseau, *Ascetics, Authority, and the Church* (1978), esp. 183–194.

22. On the Italian monastic tradition, see de Vogüé, "Saint Benoît en son temps" (1972).

23. On Gregory the Great as reconciler of ascetic technology and language with the more inclusive Augustinian ecclesiology of the three orders (ordained, ascetic, and married), see Dagens, *Saint Grégoire le Grand* (1977), esp. 312ff. For textual parallels, see Folliet, "Les trois catégories de chrétiens" (1954).

24. A well-informed discussion of the circumstances of production of the *Moralia* appears in Meyvaert, "The Enigma of Gregory the Great's *Dialogues*" (1988), 348ff.

25. On the *Moralia* see Baasten, *Pride according to Gregory the Great* (1986), and Straw, *Gregory the Great* (1988), 236ff.

26. Gregory, *Moralia in Job*, 5.20.39 (*CC* 143.245). See also 34.15.29 (*CC* 143B.1755): "For frequently, as we have said, pride is hidden and chastity is publicly known; and therefore the chastity which has been long made a show of is lost toward the end of life, because the concealed pride is sustained unamended even to the end."

27. Leyser, " 'Let me speak, let me speak' " (1990), 2.177.

28. Filastrius, *De haeresibus* 88(60).6 (*CC* 9.256).
29. See Clark, "Patrons, Not Priests" (1990).

Epilogue

1. Golb and Pritsak, *Khazarian Hebrew Documents of the Tenth Century* (1982), 107–109. Roper, *The Holy Household* (1989).
2. Williams, *Shame and Necessity* (1993).
3. Cf. Bynum, "Women's Stories, Women's Symbols."
4. See Brown, "Fundamentalism and the Control of Women" (1994).

· Bibliography ·

Primary Sources

For Christian texts, editors and place and date of publication are given only for editions that are not in the *Acta Sanctorum* or the standard Patristic series: Migne's *Patrologia*, the *Corpus Christianorum*, the *Corpus Scriptorum Ecclesiasticarum Latinorum*, and the *Sources chrétiennes*. References to biblical texts and standard classical texts are not included.

Acta Andreae: Dennis Ronald MacDonald, ed., *The Acts of Andrew and The Acts of Andrew and Matthias in the City of the Cannibals* (Atlanta: Scholar Press, 1990).

Acta Ioannis: Richard Adelbert Lipsius and Maximilian Bonnet, *Acta Apostolorum Apocrypha* vol. 2, pt. 1 (Leipzig, Mendelssohn, 1898), 151–216

Acta Matthaei: BHL 5691 (*Acta Sanctorum Sept. VI*)

Acta Pauli et Theclae: Richard Adelbert Lipsius and Maximilian Bonnet, *Acta Apostolorum Apocrypha*, vol. 1 (Leipzig: Mendelssohn, 1891), 235–272.

[De laude S. Teclae]: Michel Aubineau, "Le panégyrique de Thècle, attribué à Jean Chrysostome (*BHG* 1720), la fin retrouvée d'un texte mutilé," *AB* 93 (1975), 349–362.

Acta Thomae: Richard Adelbert Lipsius and Maximilian Bonnet, *Acta Apostolorum Apocrypha*, vol. 2, pt. 2 (Leipzig: Mendelssohn, 1903), 99–288.

Aphthonius of Antioch. *Progymnasmata:* Tr. Raymond E. Nadeau, *Speech Monographs* 19 (1952), 264–285.

Athanasius. *Peri parthenias:* Robert P. Casey, "Der dem Athanasius zugeschriebene Traktat, *Peri parthenías*," *Sitzungsberichte der Preussische Akademie der Wissenschaften. Philosophisch-historische Klasse* (Berlin, 1935), 1022–45.

Augustine. *De bono coniugali:* CSEL 41.187–231.

—— *De civitate dei:* CSEL 40.

—— *Contra Faustum:* PL 42.207–518.

—— *Confessiones:* CSEL 33.

—— *Epistulae:* CSEL 34, 44, 52, 58, 88.

—— *De haeresibus: CC* 46.283–342.

—— *De patientia: CSEL* 41.663–691.

—— *De sancta virginitate: CSEL* 41.235–302.

Carmen contra paganos: PLS 1.780–784.

Cyprian of Carthage. *De bono patientiae: CC* 3A.118–133.

Evodius of Uzala. *De Fide contra Manichaeos: PL* 42.1139–1154.

Gregory the Great. *Dialogi: SC* 251, 260, 265.

—— *Moralia in Job: CC* 143, 143A, 143B.

Gregory of Nyssa. *Vita Macrinae: PG* 46.959–1000.

Irenaeus. *Adversus haereses: PG* 7.437–1224.

Jerome. *Adversus Iovinianum: PL* 23.211–338.

—— *Adversus Helvidium: PL* 23, 183–206.

—— *Commentarii in Ezechielem: PL* 25.15–490.

—— *Epistulae: CSEL* 54, 55, 56.

Pseudo-Jerome. *De virginitate: PL* 30.165–175.

John Cassian. *Conlationes: SC* 42, 54, 64.

John Nesteutes ("The Faster"). *Sermo de poenitentia: PG* 88.1937–77.

Justin Martyr. *Apologia II Prochristianis* (*PG* 6.441–470).

Liber ad Gregoriam: PLS 3.221–256; Germain Morin, *Etudes, textes, découvertes* (Paris: Picard, 1913).

Origen. *Contra Celsum: PG* 2.641–1632.

Palladius of Helenopolis. *Dialogue on the Life of John Chrysostom: SC* 341.

Passio Sanctae Anastasiae: BHL 401; Hippolyte Delehaye, *Etude sur le legendier romain: les saints de novembre et décembre* (Brussels: Société des Bolland-istes, 1936).

Pelagius. *Epistula ad Celantiam* [authorship uncertain]: *CSEL* 56.329–356.

—— *Epistula ad Demetriadem: PL* 30.15–45.

Pseudo-Basil. *Homilia de virginitate:* David Amand and Matthieu-Charles Moons, "Une curieuse homélie grecque inédite sur la virginité adressée aux pères de famille," *Revue Bénédictine* 63 (1953), 18–69, 211–238.

Rufinus. *Apologia contra Hieronymum: CC* 20.29–123.

—— *Praefatio, Homiliae in Psalmos Origenis: CC* 20.251.

—— *Praefatio, Sententiae Sixtis: CC* 20.259.

Sextus. *Sententiae:* Henry Chadwick, *The Sentences of Sextus: A Contribution to the History of Early Christian Ethics.* Cambridge: Cambridge University Press, 1959.

Tertullian. *De patientia: CSEL* 47.1–24).

—— *De baptismo* (*CC* 1.277–295).

Vita Olympiadis: SC 13 bis.

Vita Syncleticae: PG 28.1487–1558.

Secondary Sources

Alchermes, Joseph Donella. "*Cura pro mortuis* and *cultus martyrum:* Commemoration in Rome from the Second through the Sixth Century." Diss., New York University, Institute of Fine Arts, 1989.

de Aldama, J. A. *Repertorium Pseudochrysostomicum.* Paris: CNRS, 1965.

Anderson, Graham. *Eros Sophistes: Ancient Novelists at Play.* Chico, California: Scholars Press, 1982.

Anderson, Graham. *Ancient Fiction: The Novel in the Graeco-Roman World.* London: Croom Helm, 1984.

Aubineau, Michel. "Le panégyrique de Thècle, attribué à Jean Chrysostome (*BHG* 1720), la fin retrouvée d'un texte mutilé," *AB* 93 (1975), 349–362.

Austin, J. L. *How to Do Things with Words.* Cambridge: Harvard University Press, 1962. 2nd ed., J. O. Urmson and M. Sbisa, eds. (1975).

Baasten, Matthew. *Pride according to Gregory the Great: A Study of the Moralia.* Lewiston, New York: Edwin Mellen, 1986.

Bagnall, Roger. "An Owner of Literary Papyri," *Classical Philology* 87 (1992), 137–140.

Barone, Giulia, Marina Caffiero, and Francesco Scorza Barcellona, eds. *Modelli di santità e modelli di comportamento.* Turin: Rosenberg & Sellier, 1994.

Bartsch, Shadi. *Decoding the Ancient Novel: The Reader and the Role of Description in Heliodorus and Achilles Tatius.* Princeton: Princeton University Press, 1989.

—— *Actors in the Audience: Theatricality and Doublespeak from Nero to Hadrian.* Cambridge: Harvard University Press, 1994.

Beard, Mary. "The Sexual Status of Vestal Virgins," *JRS* 70 (1980), 12–27.

Beatrice, Pier Franco. *Tradux Peccati: alle fonti della dottrina agostiniana del peccato originale.* Milan: Vita e Pensiero, 1978.

Beccaria, Augusto. *I codici miniati del periodo presalernitano (IX, X, et XIe sec.)* Rome, 1956.

Benabou, Marcel. "Pratique matrimoniale et représentation philosophique: le crépuscule des stratégies," *Annales: économies, sociétés, civilisations* 42 (1987), 1255–66.

Bilinkoff, Jodi. "Woman with a Mission: Teresa of Avila and the Apostolic Model," in Barone et al. (1994), 295–305.

Bloch, Herbert. "The Pagan Revival in the West at the End of the Fourth Century," in Arnaldo Momgliano, ed., *The Conflict between Paganism and Christianity in the Fourth Century* (Oxford: Clarendon Press, 1963), 193–218.

Boatwright, Mary Taliaferro. "Plancia Magna of Perge: Women's Roles and Status in Roman Asia Minor," in Pomeroy (1991), 249–272.

Boughton, Lynne C. "From Pious Legend to Feminist Fantasy: Distinguishing Hagiographical License from Apostolic Practice in the *Acts of Paul/Acts of Thecla*," *Journal of Religion* 71 (1991), 362–383.

Bowie, Ewen. "The Readership of Greek Novels in the Ancient World," in Tatum (1994), 435–459.

Bremmer, Jan N. "Why Did Early Christianity Attract Upper-Class Women?" in A.A.R. Bastiaensen, A. Hilhorst, and C. H. Kneepkens, eds., *Fructus Centesimus: mélanges offerts à Gerard J. M. Bartelink à l'occasion de son soixante-cinquième anniversaire* (Steenbrugis: Abbatia S. Petri, 1989), 37–47.

———— "Pauper or Patroness: the Widow in the Early Christian Church," in Bremmer and van den Bosch, (1995), 31–57.

———— and L. van den Bosch, eds. *Between Poverty and the Pyre: Monuments in the History of Widowhood.* London: Routledge, 1995.

Brenk, Frederick E., S.J. "Plutarch's *Erotikos*: The Drag Down Pulled Up," *Illinois Classical Studies* 13 (1988), 457–471.

Brooten, Bernadette J. *Women Leaders in the Ancient Synagogue.* Chico, Calif.: Scholars Press, 1982.

———— "Jewish Women's History in the Roman Period: A Task for Christian Theology," in G. W. E. Nickelsburg and George W. MacRae, eds., *Christians among Jews and Gentiles. Essays in Honor of Krister Stendahl on His Sixty-Fifth Birthday* (Philadelphia: Fortress Press, 1986), 22–30.

Brown, Karen McCarthy. "Fundamentalism and the Control of Women," in John Stratton Hawley, ed., *Fundamentalism and Gender.* New York: Oxford University Press, 1994.

Brown, Peter. *The Body and Society: Men, Women, and Sexual Renunciation in Early Christianity.* New York: Columbia University Press, 1988.

———— *Power and Persuasion in Late Antiquity: Towards a Christian Empire.* Madison: University of Wisconsin Press, 1992.

Buffière, Félix. *Eros adolescent: la pédérastie dans la Grèce antique.* Paris: Belles-Lettres, 1980.

Burrus, Virginia. *Chastity as Autonomy: Women in the Stories of Apocryphal Acts.* Lewiston, New York: Edwin Mellen, 1987.

———— "Reading Agnes: The Rhetoric of Gender in Ambrose and Prudentius," *JECS* 3 (1995), 25–46.

Bynum, Caroline Walker. "Women's Stories, Women's Symbols: A Critique of Victor Turner's Theory of Liminality," in Robert L. Moore and Frank E. Reynolds, eds., *Anthropology and the Study of Religion* (Chicago: Center for the Scientific Study of Religion, 1984), 105–125.

Cameron, Alan. "Paganism and Literature in Late Fourth Century Rome," *Christianisme et formes littéraires de l'antiquité tardive en occident. Entretiens* 23 (Geneva: Fondation Hardt, 1977), 1–30.

——— "The Date and Owners of the Esquiline Treasure: The Nature of the Evidence," *American Journal of Archaeology* 89 (1985), 135–145.

Cameron, Averil. "Redrawing the Map: Early Christian Territory after Foucault," *JRS* 76 (1986), 266–271.

——— *Christianity and the Rhetoric of Empire: The Development of Christian Discourse.* Berkeley: University of California Press, 1991.

Casey, Robert P. "Der dem Athanasius zugeschriebene Traktat, *Peri parthenías*," in *Sitzungsberichte der Preussische Akademie der Wissenschaften. Philosophisch-historische Klasse* (Berlin, 1935) 1022–45.

Castelli, Elizabeth. "Mortifying the Body, Curing the Soul: Beyond Ascetic Dualism in the *Life of Saint Syncletica*," *differences* 4.2 (1992), 134–153.

Casteras, Susan P. *Images of Victorian Womanhood in English Art.* Rutherford: Fairleigh-Dickinson University Press, 1987.

Chadwick, Henry. *The Sentences of Sextus: A Contribution to the History of Early Christian Ethics.* Cambridge: Cambridge University Press, 1959.

Chang, Jung. *Wild Swans: Three Daughters of China.* New York: Simon and Schuster, 1991.

Clark, Elizabeth A. *Ascetic Piety and Women's Faith: Essays on Late Ancient Christianity.* Lewiston, New York: Edwin Mellen, 1986.

——— "Ascetic Renunciation and Feminine Advancement: A Paradox of Late Ancient Christianity," *Anglican Theological Review* 63 (1981), 240–257. Reprt. Clark (1986), 175–208.

——— "Authority and Humility: A Conflict of Values in Fourth-Century Female Monasticism," *Byzantinische Forschungen* 9 (1985), 17–33. Reprt. Clark (1986), 209–228.

——— *The Life of Melania the Younger: Introduction, Translation and Commentary.* Lewiston, New York: Edwin Mellen, 1984.

——— "Patrons, Not Priests: Gender and Power in Late Ancient Christianity," *Gender and History* 2 (1990), 253–273.

Cloke, Gillian. *"This Female Man of God": Women and Spiritual Power in the Patristic Age, AD 350–450.* London: Routledge, 1995.

Consolino, Franca Ela. "Dagli *exempla* ad un esempio di comportamento cristiano: il *De exhortatione virginitatis* di Ambrogio," *Rivista storica italiana* 94 (1982), 455–477.

——— "*Veni huc a Libano*: la *sponsa* del Cantico dei Cantici come modello per le vergini negli scritti esortatori di Ambrogio," *Athenaeum* n.s. 62 (1984), 399–415.

———— "Modelli di comportamento e modi di sanctificazione per l'aristocrazia femminile d'Occidente," in Andrea Giardina, ed., *Società romana e impero tardoantico*, vol. 1, *Istituzioni, ceti, economia* (Bari: Laterza, 1986), 273–306.

———— "Modelli di santità femminile nelle più antiche Passioni romane," *Augustinianum* 24 (1984), 83–113.

Cooper, Kate. "Insinuations of Womanly Influence: An Aspect of the Christianization of the Roman Aristocracy," *JRS* 82 (1992), 150–164.

———— "Concord and Martyrdom: Gender, Community, and the Uses of Christian Perfection." Diss., Princeton University, 1993.

———— "An(n)ianus of Celeda and the Latin Readers of John Chrysostom," *Studia Patristica* 27 (1993), 249–255.

Courcelle, Pierre. "La vision cosmique de S. Benoît," *REAug* 13 (1967), 97–117.

———— *Lecteurs païens et lecteurs chrétiens de l'énéide*, vol. 1, *Les témoignages littéraires*. Paris: Institut de France, 1984.

Cracco Ruggini, Lellia. *Il paganesimo romano tra religione e politica (384–394 d.C.): per una reinterpretazione del Carmen contra paganos*. Rome: Accademia Nazionale dei Lincei, 1979.

Croke, Brian, and Jill Harries, *Religious Conflict in Fourth-Century Rome; A Documentary Study*. Sydney: Sydney University Press, 1982.

Culler, Jonathan. "Readers and Reading: Reading as a Woman," in his *On Deconstruction: Theory and Criticism after Structuralism* (Ithaca: Cornell University Press, 1982), 43–64.

Dagens, Claude. *Saint Grégoire le Grand: culture et expérience chrétiennes*. Paris: Etudes Augustiniennes, 1977.

Davies, Bronwyn, and Rom Harré. "Positioning: The Discursive Production of Selves," *Journal for the Theory of Social Behavior* 20.1 (1990), 43–63.

Davies, Stevan L. *The Revolt of the Widows: The Social World of the Apocryphal Acts*. Carbondale: Southern Illinois University Press, 1980.

Dawson, David. *Allegorical Readers and Cultural Revision in Ancient Alexandria*. Berkeley: University of California Press, 1992.

Douglas, Mary. "Social Preconditions of Enthusiasm and Heterodoxy," in *Forms of Symbolic Action: Proceedings of the 1969 Annual Meeting of the American Ethnological Society* (Seattle: American Ethnological Society, 1969).

Dufourcq, Albert. *Etude sur les Gesta martyrum romains* (1882–1910). Reprt. Rome: Ecole Française de Rome et d'Athènes, 1988, 5 vols.

Egger, Brigitte. "Zu den Frauenrollen im griechischen Roman: Die Frau als Heldin und Leserin," *GCN* 1 (1988), 33–66.

—— "Women and Marriage in the Greek Novels: The Boundaries of Romance," in Tatum (1994), 260–280.

Elm, Susanna. *Virgins of God: The Making of Asceticism in Late Antiquity.* Oxford: Clarendon Press, 1994.

Elsom, Helen E. "Callirhoe: Displaying the Phallic Woman," in Amy Richlin, ed., *Pornography and Representation in Greece and Rome* (Oxford: Oxford University Press, 1992), 212–230.

Evans, Robert F. *Four Letters of Pelagius.* London: Black, 1968.

Felson-Rubin, Nancy. *Regarding Penelope: From Character to Poetics.* Princeton: Princeton University Press, 1994.

Festugière, A. J. "Initiée par l'époux," in his *Hermétisme et mystique païenne* (Paris: Aubier-Montaigne, 1967), 322–333.

Flacelière, Robert, ed. *Plutarque: oeuvres morales,* vol. 10, *Dialogue sur l'amour.* Paris: Belles-Lettres, 1980.

Folliet, Georges. "Les trois catégories de chrétiens: survie d'un thème augustinien," *L'Année théologique augustinienne* 14 (1954), 81–96.

Foucault, Michel. *Histoire de la sexualité,* vol. 3, *Le souci de soi.* Paris: Gallimard, 1984. Tr. R. Hurley, *The Care of the Self* (New York: Pantheon, 1985).

Francis, James A. *Subversive Virtue: Asceticism and Authority in the Second-Century Pagan World.* University Park: Pennsylvania State University Press, 1995.

Frye, Northrop. *The Secular Scripture: A Study of the Structure of Romance.* Cambridge: Harvard University Press, 1976.

Gager, John G. "Body-Symbols and Social Reality: Resurrection, Incarnation, and Asceticism in Early Christianity," *Religion* 12 (1982), 345–363.

de Gaiffier, Baldouin. "Un prologue hagiographique hostile au décret de Gélase?" *AB* 82 (1964), 341–353.

Garnsey, Peter. "Aspects of the Decline of the Urban Aristocracy in the Empire," *ANRW* 2.1 (1974), 227–252.

Gleason, Maud W. *Making Men: Sophists and Self-Presentation in Ancient Rome.* Princeton: Princeton University Press, 1995.

Goffman, Erving. *The Presentation of Self in Everyday Life.* New York: Anchor Books, 1959.

—— *Frame Analysis.* New York: Harper and Row, 1974.

Golb, Norman, and Omeljan Pritsak. *Khazarian Hebrew Documents of the Tenth Century.* Ithaca: Cornell University Press, 1982.

Goldhill, Simon. *Foucault's Virginity: Ancient Erotic Fiction and the History of Sexuality.* Cambridge: Cambridge University Press, 1995.

Gordini, G. D. "Origine e sviluppo del monachesimo a Roma," *Gregorianum* 37 (1956), 220–260.

Harris, Willaim V. *Ancient Literacy.* Cambridge: Harvard University Press, 1989.

Halperin, David M. "Historicizing the Seuxual Body: Sexual Preferences and Erotic Identities in the Pseudo-Lucianic *Erōtes,*" in Domna C. Stanton, ed., *Discourses of Sexuality: From Aristotle to AIDS* (Ann Arbor: University of Michigan Press, 1992), 236–261.

Hickey, Anne Ewing. *Women of the Roman Aristocracy as Christian Monastics.* Ann Arbor: UMI Research Press, 1987.

Holder, A. *Die Handschriften der Landesbibliothek Karlsruhe,* vol. 1, *Die Reichenauer Handschriften.* Leipzig, 1906.

Holum, Kenneth. *Theodosian Empresses: Women and Imperial Dominion in Late Antiquity.* Berkeley: University of California Press, 1982.

Hopkins, Keith. *Death and Renewal.* Cambridge: Cambridge University Press, 1983.

Hunter, David. "Resistance to the Virginal Ideal in Late Fourth-Century Rome: The Case of Jovinian," *Theological Studies* 48 (1987), 45–64.

——— "Helvidius, Jovinian and the Virginity of Mary in Late Fourth-Century Rome," *JECS* 1 (1993), 47–71.

Janssens, Jos, S.J. *Vita e morte del cristiano negli epitaffi di Roma anteriori al sec. VII.* Rome: Università Gregoriana Editrice, 1981.

Kaestli, Jean-Daniel. "Response [to Virginia Burrus]," *Semeia* 38 (1986), 119–131.

Kampen, Natalie Boymel. "Between Public and Private: Women as Historical Subjects in Roman Art," in Pomeroy, (1991), 218–248.

Kaster, Robert A. *Guardians of Language: The Grammarian and Society in Late Antiquity.* Berkeley: University of California Press, 1988.

Kelly, J.N.D. *Jerome: His Life, Writings, and Controversies.* New York: Harper and Row, 1975.

Kirkby, Helen. "The Scholar and His Public," in Margaret Gibson, ed., *Boethius: His Life, Thought, and Influence* (Oxford: Blackwell, 1981), 44–69.

Konstan, David. "Frankness, Flattery, and Friendship." Paper at annual meeting of Society of Biblical Literature, November 1992.

——— "The Invention of Fiction." Paper at annual meeting of Society of Biblical Literature, November 1993.

——— *Sexual Symmetry: Love in the Ancient Novel and Related Genres.* Princeton: Princeton University Press, 1994.

Kraemer, Ross S. "The Conversion of Women to Ascetic Forms of Christianity," *Signs: Journal of Women in Culture and Society* 6 (1980), 298–307.

—— *Her Share of the Blessings: Women's Religions Among Pagans, Jews and Christians in the Greco-Roman World.* New York: Oxford University Press, 1992.

Kuttner, Ann. "Venus in the World of Constantine." Manuscript.

Lamberton, Robert. *Homer the Theologian: Neoplatonist Allegorical Reading and the Growth of the Epic Tradition.* Berkeley: University of California Press, 1986.

Lenain de Tillemont, Sebastien. *Mémoires pour servir à l'histoire ecclésiastique des six premiers siècles; justifiez par les citations des auteurs originaux,* vol. 5, Paris, 1698.

Levick, Barbara. "Concordia at Rome," in R.A.G. Carson and Colin M. Kraay, eds., *Scripta Nummaria Romana: Essays Presented to Humphrey Sutherland* (London: Spink, 1978), 217–233.

Leyser, Conrad. " 'Let me speak, let me speak': Vulnerability and Authority in Gregory's Homilies on Ezekiel," in *Gregorio Magno e il suo tempo: XIX incontro di studiosi dell'antichità cristiana in collaborazione con l'Ecole française de Rome.* Rome, Institutum Patristit cum "Augustinianum" (1991), 2.169–182.

—— "*Lectio divina, oratio pura:* Rhetoric and the Techniques of Asceticism in the *Conferences* of John Cassian," in Barone et al. (1994), 79–105.

Literacy in the Roman World. Ann Arbor: *Journal of Roman Archaeology,* 1991.

Limberis, Vasiliki. *Divine Heiress: The Virgin Mary and the Creation of Christian Constantinople.* London: Routledge, 1994.

MacDonald, Dennis Ronald. *The Legend and the Apostle: The Battle for Paul in Story and Canon.* Philadelphia: Westminster, 1983.

—— *The Acts of Andrew and the Acts of Andrew and Matthias in the City of the Cannibals.* Atlanta: Scholars Press, 1990.

—— *Christianizing Homer: "The Odyssey," Plato, and "The Acts of Andrew."* New York: Oxford University Press, 1994.

MacMullen, Ramsay. *Christianizing the Roman Empire (A.D. 100–400).* New Haven: Yale University Press, 1984.

—— *Corruption and the Decline of Rome.* New Haven: Yale University Press, 1988.

Markus, Robert. *The End of Ancient Christianity.* Cambridge: Cambridge University Press, 1990.

Martimort, A. G. *Les diaconesses: essai historique.* Rome: Edizioni Liturgiche, 1982.

Martindale, John, and A. H. M. Jones, *Prosopography of the Later Roman Empire,* 3 vols. Cambridge: Cambridge University Press, 1971–1992.

Matthews, John. "Symmachus and the Oriental Cults," *JRS* 83 (1973), 175–195.

—— "The Historical Setting of the *Carmen contra paganos* (cod. par. lat. 8084)," *Historia* 19 (1970), 464–470.

McLynn, Neil B. *Ambrose of Milan: Church and Court in a Christian Capital.* Berkeley: University of California Press, 1994.

McShane, Philip. *La romanitas et le pape Léon le Grand: l'apport culturel des institutions impériales à la formation des structures ecclésiastiques.* Tournai: Desclée, 1979.

Merkelbach, Reinhold. *Roman und Mysterium in der Antike.* Munich-Berlin: C. H. Beck, 1962.

Meyvaert, Paul. "The Enigma of Gregory the Great's *Dialogues:* A Response to Francis Clark," *JEH* 39 (1988), 335–381.

Monachesi, Maria. "Arnobio Iuniore ed una sua possibilità agiografica," *Bulletino di studi storico-religiosi* 1 (1921), 96–109; 2.2 (1922), 18–27; 2.3 (1922), 66–125.

Morin, Germain. "Un traité inédit d'Arnobe le Jeune: le *Libellus ad Gregoriam*," *RB* 27 (1910), 153–171. Repr. in his *Etudes, textes, découvertes* (Paris: Picard, 1913).

—— "Fragments pélagiens inédits du manuscrit 954 de Vienne," *RB* 34 (1922), 265–275.

Murphy, F. X. *Rufinus of Aquileia: His Life and Works.* Washington: Catholic University of America Studies in Medieval History, n.s. 6, 1945.

Nightingale, H. W. "The Folly of Praise: Plato's Critique of Encomiastic Discourse in the *Lysis* and *Symposium*," *CQ* 43 (1993), 112–130.

Nock, A. D. *Conversion: The Old and the New in Religion from Alexander the Great to Augustine of Hippo.* Oxford: Oxford University Press, 1993, reprt. 1961.

North, Helen. *Sophrosyne: Self-Knowledge and Restraint in Classical Antiquity.* Ithaca: Cornell University Press, 1966.

Parsons, Talcott. *The Social System.* Glencoe: Free Press, 1951.

Patmore, Coventry. *The Angel in the House.* London: J. W. Parker, 1854. Reprt. 1979, Arden Library.

Perry, Ben Edwin. *The Ancient Romances: A Literary-Historical Account of Their Origins.* Berkeley: University of California Press, 1967.

Perkins, Judith. "The Apocryphal Acts and the Early Christian Martyrdom," *Arethusa* 18 (1985), 211–230.

—— *The Suffering Self: Pain and Narrative Representation in the Early Christian Era.* London: Routledge, 1995.

Pervo, Richard I. *Profit with Delight: The Literary Genre of the Acts of the Apostles.* Philadelphia: Fortress Press, 1987.

Pomeroy, Sarah B., ed. *Women's History and Ancient History.* Chapel Hill: University of North Carolina Press, 1991.

Polara, Giovanni. "Le iscrizioni sul cippo tombale di Vezzio Agorio Pretestato," *Vichiana* 4 (1967), 264–289.

Rabinowitz, Nancy Sorkin, and Amy Richlin, eds. *Feminist Theory and the Classics.* New York: Routledge, 1993.

Raditsa, Leo Ferrero. "Augustus' Legislation Concerning Marriage, Procreation, Love Affairs and Adultery," *ANRW* 2.13 (1980), 278–339.

Radway, Janice. *Reading the Romance: Women, Patriarchy, and Popular Literature.* Chapel Hill: University of North Carolina Press, 1984.

Rajak, Tessa, and D. Noy. "*Archisynagogoi:* Office, Title, and Social Status in the Greco-Jewish Synagoogue," *JRS* 83 (1993), 75–93.

Reardon, B. P., ed. *Collected Ancient Greek Novels.* Berkeley: University of California Press, 1989.

Richlin, Amy. "The Ethnographer's Dilemma and the Dream of a Lost Golden Age," in Rabinowitz and Richlin (1993), 272–303.

Rohde, Erwin. *Der Griechische Roman und seine Vorlaufer.* Leipzig, 1876.

Roper, Lyndal. *The Holy Household: Women and Morals in Reformation Augsburg.* Oxford: Oxford University Press, 1989.

Rousseau, Philip. *Ascetics, Authority, and the Church in the Age of Jerome and Cassian.* Oxford: Oxford University Press, 1978.

Ruether, Rosemary Radford. "Misogynism and Virginal Feminism in the Fathers of the Church," in Ruether, ed., *Religion and Sexism: Images of Women in the Jewish and Christian Traditions* (New York: Simon and Schuster, 1974), 150–183.

Saller, Richard. "Corporal Punishment, Authority, and Obedience in the Roman Household," in Beryl Rawson, ed., *Marriage, Divorce, and Children in Ancient Rome* (Oxford: Clarendon Press, 1991), 144–165.

Saller, Richard, and Brent Shaw. "Tombstones and Roman Family Relations in the Principate," *JRS* 74 (1984), 124–156.

Schäferdiek, Knut. "The Acts of John," in Schneemelcher (1992).

——— "The Manichaean Collection of Apocryphal Acts Ascribed to Leucius Charinus," in Schneemelcher (1992).

Schiffrin, Deborah. *Approaches to Discourse* (Oxford: Blackwell, 1994).

Schneemelcher, Wilhelm, ed. *New Testament Apocrypha,* tr. R.M.L. Wilson et al. Cambridge, Eng.: James Clarke, 1992.

Scott, Joan W. *Gender and the Politics of History.* New York: Columbia University Press, 1989.

Searle, J. R. *Expression and Meaning.* Cambridge: Cambridge University Press, 1979.

Sesser, Stan. *The Lands of Charm and Cruelty.* New York: Vintage, 1994.

Shaw, Brent. "The Passion of Perpetua," *Past and Present* 139 (1993), 3–45.

Shelton, Jo-Ann. "Pliny the Younger and the Ideal Wife," *Classica et Medievalia* 41 (1990), 163–186.

Shelton, Kathleen J. *The Esquiline Treasure.* London: British Museum Publications, 1981.

——— "The Esquiline Treasure: The Nature of the Evidence," *American Journal of Archaeology* 89 (1985), 147–155.

Sicari, Amalia. *Prostituzione e tutela giuridica della schiava: un problema di politica legislativa nell'impero romano.* Bari: Cacucci, 1991.

Söder, Rosa. *Die apokryphen Apostelgeschichlte und die romanhafte Literatur der Antike.* Stuttgart: W. Kohlhammer, 1932.

Souter, A. "The 'Acta Pauli' etc. in Tertullian," *JTS* 25 (1924), 292.

Stephens, Susan A. "Who Read the Ancient Novels?" in Tatum, (1994), 405–418.

Straw, Carole. *Gregory the Great: Perfection in Imperfection.* Berkeley: University of California Press, 1988.

Tannen, Deborah. *You Just Don't Understand: Women and Men in Conversation.* New York: Ballantine, 1991.

Tatum, James, ed. *The Search for the Ancient Novel.* Baltimore: Johns Hopkins University Press, 1994.

Theissen, Gerd. *The Sociology of Early Palestinian Christianity.* Philadelphia: Fortress Press, 1978.

Tiblietti, Carlo. *Verginità e matrimonio in antichi scrittori cristiani.* Rome: Bretschneider, 1983.

Toubert, Pierre. "La théorie du mariage chez les moralistes carolingiens," in *Il matrimonio nella società altomedievale* (Spoleto: Centro Italiano di Studi sull'Alto Medievo, 1977), 1.233–285.

Treggiari, Susan. *Roman Marriage: Iusti Coniuges from the Time of Cicero to the Time of Ulpian.* Oxford: Clarendon Press, 1991.

Valantasis, Richard. "A Theory of the Social Function of Asceticism," in Valantasis and Vincent L. Wimbush, eds., *Asceticism* (New York: Oxford University Press, 1995), 544–552.

Van Geytenbeek, A. C. *Musonius Rufus and Greek Diatribe.* Assen: Van Garcum, 1962.

Van Loveren, A.E.D. "Once Again: 'The Monk and the Martyr,' Saint Anthony and Saint Macrina," *Studia Patristica* 17 (1982), 2.528–538.

van Ommeslaeghe, Florent. "Jean Chrysostome en conflit avec l'impératrice Eudoxie: le dossier et les origines d'une légende," *AB* 97 (1979), 131–159.

Vauchez, André. "Saints admirables et saints imitables: les fonctions de l'hagiographie ont-elles changé aux derniers siècles du moyen âge?" in *Les fonctions des saints dans le monde occidental (IIIe-XIIIe siècle): actes du colloque organisé par l'Ecole française de Rome avec le concours de l'Université de Rome "La Sapienza." Roma, 27–29 octobre 1988* (Rome: Ecole Française, 1991), 161–172.

Vernant, J.-P. "Hestia-Hermes: The Religious Expression of Space and Movement in Ancient Greece," in his *Myth and Thought among the Greeks* (London: Routledge, 1983), 127–175.

Veyne, Paul. "La famille et l'amour sous le haut-empire romain," *Annales:* 33 (1978), 35–63.

Vinaver, Eugène. *The Rise of Romance.* Cambridge, Eng.: Brewer, 1971.

de Vogüé, Adalbert. "Saint Benoît en son temps: règles italiennes et règles provençales au VIe siècle," *Regulae Benedicti Studia* 1 (1972), 169–193.

von Kellenbach, Katharina. *Anti-Judaism in Feminist Religious Writings.* Atlanta: Scholars Press, 1994.

Wesseling, Berber. "The Audience of the Ancient Novels," *GCN* 1 (1988), 67–79.

Williams, Bernard. *Shame and Necessity.* Berkeley: University of California Press, 1993.

Wimbush, Vincent L., ed. *Ascetic Behavior in Greco-Roman Antiquity: A Sourcebook.* Minneapolis: Fortress Press, 1990.

Winkler, John J. *Auctor and Actor: A Narratological Reading of Apuleius' The Golden Ass.* Berkeley: University of California Press, 1985.

—— *The Constraints of Desire: The Anthropology of Sex and Gender in Ancient Greece.* New York: Routledge, 1990.

Zeitlin, Froma. "The Poetics of *Erōs*: Nature, Art, and Imitation in Longus' *Daphnis and Chloe*," in David M. Halperin, John J. Winkler, and Zeitlin, eds., *Before Sexuality: The Construction of Erotic Experience in the Ancient Greek World* (Princeton: Princeton University Press, 1990), 417–464.

· Index ·